Your Natural Up

Human Hardwiring and the Alexander Technique

By
Marjean McKenna

Illustrated by
Christopher Neville

Your Natural Up

Human Hardwiring and the Alexander Technique

Produced and Illustrated by Christopher Neville.

Printed in the United States of America
First Printing January, 2017
ISBN-13: 978-0692759486
ISBN-10: 0692759484

Salt Lake City, Utah 84102

www.yournaturalup.com

Dedicated
to
Frank Ottiwell

Notes on Style

Spelling
Brainstem spelled as one word (as per anatomist Frank Netter).
Semi-supine (with hyphen).
Sit bones (two words). Variation of sitz bones, sitting bones, and ischial tuberosities.
Well-being (with hyphen).

Italicized: *direction, inhibition, monkey, position of mechanical advantage,*
and *use* (as a noun).

Abbreviations (without periods)
AO joint = atlanto-occipital joint.
AT = Alexander Technique. (Alexander's technique, the Technique)
FM = Frederick Matthias Alexander.
AR = Albert Redden Alexander, FM's brother.
HNB = head neck back (relationship) = all one thing.

Word choices and definitions
Crawling refers to moving on 'all fours.' Historically that movement had been dubbed "creeping," which today refers to belly crawling.

Hip bone often is used to refer specifically to the prominent iliac crest in front. In this book it will refer to the "innominate bone," the fusion of six bones, which together with the sacrum & coccyx form the *pelvis*.

Footnotes are at the bottom of the page where they appear in the text.

Endnotes, beginning on page 165, are listed by chapter.

Credits for illustrations and photographs are at the back.

I welcome corrections and clarifications and apologize for all errors. Please set me straight. Many of the quotes are "general knowledge." The author has made every effort to contact all copyright owners and is happy to amend acknowledgments in later editions of the book.

Table of Contents

Your Natural Up

Introduction

Your Natural Up is a book for everyone—for all head-bearing upright humans who might want to use themselves better. Its premise is that if adults retain the skills of an infant, specifically locomotion on all 4's, they won't suffer back pain or loss of stature as they age. The book explains the evolutionary and developmental underpinnings of the *Alexander Technique*, which addresses the "use" of the self.

The *central nerve cord* is the major organizing structure of the human body. It is present in every bilaterally symmetrical animal and is the first recognizable structure in the human embryo. In vertebrates the nerve cord preceded the bone that now encases it by millions of years. It is hardwired to be in the back of the body, with its leading end extending into the skull. It is delicate, yet its well-being is paramount. Now oriented vertically, its well-being may require conscious intervention from most of us. That is the theme of this book.

In the late 1800s the aspiring Australian actor, FM Alexander, suffered voice problems. In searching for the cause, he discovered that whenever he even thought of speaking he would pull his head back and down, interfering with the relationship of his head to his neck and back, shortening his stature, and rendering him less capable in myriad ways. During nine years of self-observation, he not only solved his own voice problems, but also happened upon some far-reaching truths.

His work, the *Alexander Technique*, addresses the integrity of the back and its role as the mainstay of the body's axis and protector of that delicate nerve cord. Our evolution to vertical was not a mistake. Verticality with such a big head on top, however, is a setup for problems unless we can retain that 4-legged organization of head leading and body following. How we "use" ourselves affects how we function and, over time, how we are structured.

Watching toddlers, you can see how every single cell of the brainpan wants to be up. It's effortless—those heads do not appear heavy.

*The use of the self** has far-reaching ramifications. In fact, the "right *use* of one's body might well be a basic factor in preventive medicine."[1] The first medical doctor to become an AT teacher asserted that habitual *misuse* "eventually finds its expression in a posture or in a limited repertoire of postures, which come to dominate a person's character. In small and unobtrusive ways we become enslaved to our past."[2] So, a change in stature can lead to a change in who you are—something that can be easily witnessed in acting.

I contend that cultivating the skills of an infant and learning to crawl will organize us in a manner that honors the integrity of our backs and the well-being of our nerve cords. By understanding your hardwiring, you will understand the human relationship to other vertebrates and *your natural up*. This book addresses the simplicity of the Alexander Technique through the evolutionary and developmental sciences behind it.

---

* *The Use of the Self* is the title of Alexander's third book.

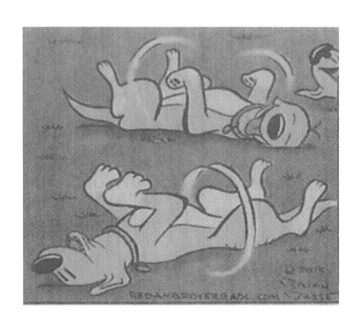

CHAPTER 1

The Primary Axis

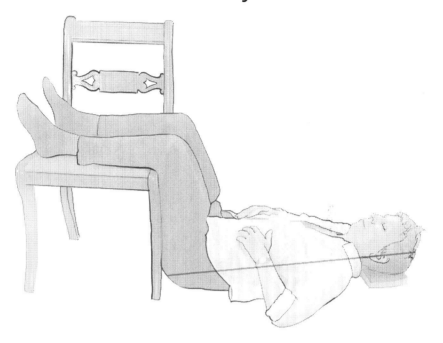

In the history of life on Earth, by far the most popular choice of body shape for animals that move has been elongate *bilateral symmetrically** with a food-seeking mouth at the leading end. A central nervous system, running the length of these organisms parallel to the gut, gradually swelled at the leading end, as sense organs collected there to assist the mouth in the pursuit of food. This swelling of the nerve cord, an ancestral brain, is dubbed the *brainstem* and is hardwired to go first in movement.

This *central nerve cord* defines the *primary axis* of the human body. It is represented in this drawing by the straight line from the skull to the bottom of the torso. Because the human central nerve cord is encased in skull and spine, the human primary axis can be considered to be the head and torso together—the evolutionary equivalent to the primary axis of other bilaterally symmetrical animals whose heads are not separate from the rest of their bodies.

---

* All existing bilaterally symmetrical animals, 35 of 38 phyla, have a common ancestor, dubbed *Urbilateria*. Most imagined extra terrestrials also exhibit this body plan.

Bilaterally symmetrical animals all exhibit an organizational movement pattern of *head leading and body following*. Our verticality doesn't change this evolutionary movement organization, which is illustrated in photographs and drawings throughout this book.

Two fish-like pre-vertebrate ancestors, Amphioxus and Haikouella, with imagined central nerve cords and brainstems sketched in.

Head leads and the body follows

We are hardwired to follow the head in movement. The horizontal movement of fish as well as our 4-legged vertebrate cousins exerts a lengthening influence on their entire structures. This length ensures the well-being of their nerve cords and the volume of their containers. Crawling replicates this horizontal movement.

The leading end of the central nerve cord, the *brainstem*, connects with the sense organs and orchestrates things like balance, breathing, and digestion. The German scientist Rudolf Magnus identified "a *primary control* located in the brainstem of vertebrate animals that organized their movement." FM Alexander adopted this term, "primary control," to describe the importance of the head/neck/back relationship to overall well-being.

It is the brainstem that leads movement—we are hardwired for this leading end to go first. When the brainstem is denied its functional pre-eminence, we ignore millions of years of evolution and set the stage for serious mal-coordination.

Back Back

A second observation about the hardwiring of the human central nerve cord is its *dorsal* position in the back.* In our uprightness the nerve cord must retain its place in the back. This means that the head and vertebral column that encase the nerve cord must stay more or less on the same plane.

Return to the sketch at the beginning of this chapter to notice not just the *primary axis*, but also the surface area of contact between my head and back with the floor. This surface area defines the *plane of the back*, the part of the body

---

* The nerve cord of many elongate symmetrical animals, insects for instance, is ventral—in the front.

Seabiscuit's back, in the back, clearly organizes his whole body.

that should stay back in movement. In the pictures of athletes throughout this book you will see the obvious planes of their backs. The back and the back of the head should remain on a single plane, supporting the Alexander directive, *"Back back."**

For our fish-like predecessors who lived buoyantly in water, gravity was not a problem. Over evolutionary time, cartilage was deposited around the delicate dorsal nerve cord, first to protect it and then to provide anchor for muscles. In most fish, cartilage developed into bone, making their bodies strong enough to hold shape on land.

---

* The Alexander direction, "Back back," was purportedly coined by Patrick Macdonald.

Evolving further, fins became limbs that would be strong enough to lift the primary axis off the ground. On land, the heads of amphibians, reptiles, and mammals continued to lead, lengthening their entire segmented spinal structures with every step. The spine remained in back (on top) and clearly organized the entire body. The bony vertebrate central skeleton of head and spine has become so dominant that it's easy to forget its ancestral function of protecting the nerve cord.

Watch apes in the zoo. Although they move with their spines closer to a 45° angle to earth, their backs are nevertheless still on top, in back. Watch a toddler keep the back of his head in line with the rest of his back. Now upright, most adult humans may need to consciously consider the nerve cord's place in the back. *Back back* was never a problem until we became vertical.

The back of the head, the occiput, is the head of the back, and should therefore stay back with the rest of the back. The joint connecting head to neck should obviously also stay back.

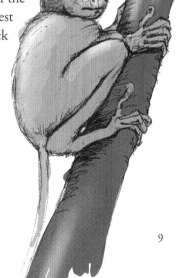

9

Look at the image of the great quarterback Joe Montana on the opposite page. How clearly his whole back stays in the back of his body! Note the line from the sit bones to the back of his eyes.

The golfer addressing the ball must keep the whole plane of his back in the back as he prepares his swing, which will wrap him around his primary axis. Notice how he aims headward (and tail-ward) with his primary axis. In maintaining length and breadth, he will develop consistency in his swing, while slack in the mainstay will invite inconsistency.

Golfer Adam Scott addressing the ball.
Check out the integrity of his primary axis.

Quarterback Joe Montana's whole back stays back as he prepares to pass.

Jackie Joyner-Kersee's back and head maintain the plane of her back.

Rafael Nadal's primary axis spirals around itself.

Embryonic Development

As the *first recognizable structure* of the human embryo, the dorsal nerve cord defines the primary axis, running its length with a head-to-tail hierarchy.* All development along the nerve cord starts at the leading end and ripples down sequentially from head to tail. The chart on the opposite page compares vertebrate embryos at approximately day seven. Note the nerve cord's primacy and how it defines the back of each embryo—each body is built around the nerve cord.

Look at how amazingly similar the embryos are—tiny tweaks in timing of developmental events lead to vastly different adult forms. Changes in development are the mechanism of evolution.†

The flexible rod of cartilage that holds the shape of our fish-like predecessors, the *notochord*, is functional in humans only in the early embryo, but it retains its *spacer function* by morphing into the spine's cushioning discs during development. When the human spine is horizontal and not bearing weight (as in lying down), the discs can absorb bodily fluids and become more taut to create a bit more space between each and every vertebra. This lengthens the entire spinal structure and increases the volume of the torso—everything inside the body functions better with more space.

Look once more at the drawing that began this chapter and appreciate the well-being fostered by lying down in this manner.

In the next chapter we discuss our evolution to verticality and the problems encountered when we got there.

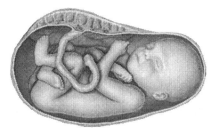

Near-term human fetus—note the clarity of the primary axis.

---

* The nerve cord is actually a tube whose anterior end is destined to fold into the brain. Residing inside the skull, the brainstem is the leading end of the nerve cord.

† All animals share the same genetic toolkit for making bodies.

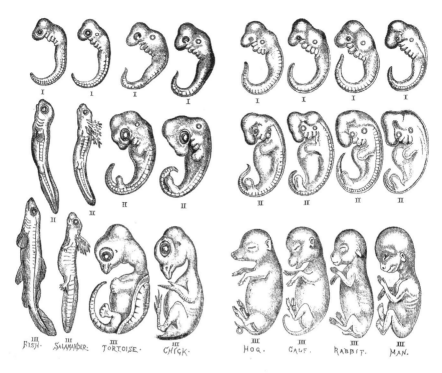

I I I I   I I I I

II II II II   II II II II

III   III   III   III   III   III   III   III
FISH· SALAMANDER· TORTOISE· CHICK·   HOG. CALF. RABBIT. MAN.

Haeckel's controversial 1874 chart comparing eight vertebrate embryos.
Look at the astonishing similarity of ROW ONE at approximately day seven.*

---

* Haeckel has fudged the relative timing to highlight the early-stage similarities. Molecular biology now backs the comparisons he made.

15

Okamoto Yoko Shihan, 6th dan, preparing to lead an aikido class.

CHAPTER 2

Verticality

Verticality came in two stages—sitting first, then standing.

The earliest primates had strong vertical spinal columns in almost any relationship with gravity. In their arboreal habitat they sat vertically and branch-walked in many variations of upright. "All major groups of non-human primates include species that sit or sleep in an upright position."[1] When our more immediate primate ancestors moved to the ground, their spines were already strong in the vertical—we were comfortable in upright long before we became "bipedal," walking on two feet. The infant, likewise, sits before he stands, with the sit bones functioning as part of the back to support the entire primary axis.

Evolving to vertical was no evolutionary mistake, but upright human beings must continue to lead with their heads to maintain the primary axes of their bodies. The *brainstem*, the specialized head-end of the ancestral nerve cord, the focus of Alexander's *primary control*, is hardwired to go first in movement. In verticality, it wants to be "up." The entire central nerve cord dislikes getting pinched or chronically bent out of shape. One must not let the heavy head or the relationship of head to neck interfere with the well-being of that delicate nerve cord.

In verticality, whether sitting or standing, *upthrust** comes through contact with the ground. The sit bones and the feet are our contact points for conducting upthrust; trust of this support allows the sense organs to get as high as possible. Our eyes and nose face forward while the *direction that lengthens the spine* is now *up*, toward the crown of the head.

---

* Gravity's equal but opposite force.

Primate branch-walking. The vertebral column became strong in the upright before our immediate ancestors moved to the ground.

The central nerve cord has a series of paired nerves along its length—the "spinal nerves" reside outside the skull, while those received by the brainstem inside the skull are the "cranial nerves," whose leading two pairs bring in sensory information from the nose and eyes.

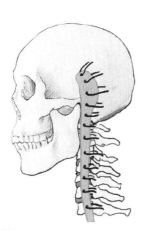

Ancestral nerve cord extending into the skull as the brainstem. Schematics show paired cranial nerves inside the skull and the identical wiring of paired spinal nerves further down.

Madagascar monkey demonstrating a vertical spine in sitting.

Verticality presented a delicate balancing act. Toddlers do it well, but adults often have to consciously remember to follow their heads. So, how do we retain that headward intentionality in upright? How do we manage the weight of the head without impinging upon its range of motion? How does the back maintain its primacy, rotated 90° from its original horizontal orientation? How do we prevent the girth and weight of the back bones from overshadowing the delicate nervous system that they encase?

The hole at the base of the skull through which the nerve cord passes is narrow with thin, almost sharp, edges of bone threatening the nerve cord's well-being.

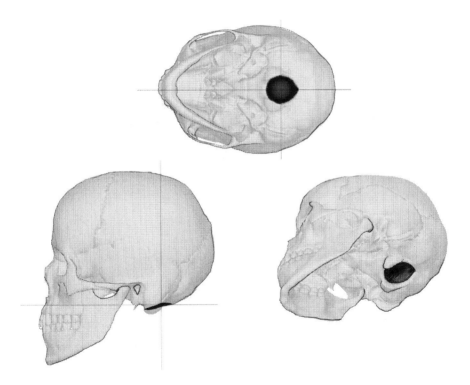

Three views of the human skull show the foramen magnum, the hole at the base of the skull through which the nerve cord passes.

Look at how small that opening is! Its bony edges are thin, almost sharp.

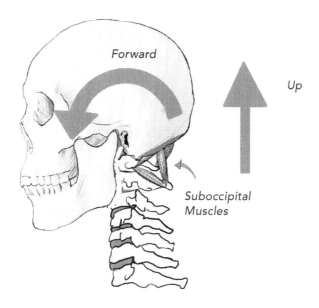

Forward refers to the pivot of the head at the top of the spine.
Up refers to the headward lengthening of the back.

In verticality, the back, including the head, must maintain the same relationship of parts that organizes a horizontal body. The head pivots forward at the *atlanto-occipital joint* at the top of the spine. The *suboccipital muscles*, which span that joint, must remain free of tension so that they can counterbalance the weight of the head. If the neck muscles are tensed, the head will become a dead weight, losing its poise and diminishing stature—the stretch of the suboccipital muscles is crucial for biomechanical poise and well-being.

The inner ear's balance organs automatically bring the plane of the base of the skull, the *brainpan*, to level. Nerves to and from the eyes, ears, and nose all follow a horizontal trajectory toward the brainstem, which is just above the brainpan. Every single cell of the brainstem and the nerve web feeding into it wants to be up, balanced, and first in movement. The rest of the body is subordinate to this area. Watch toddlers, who are just learning to walk, chase after their heads—their feet are at service to the head, while their legs "just tag along."[2]

We must protect that delicate dorsal nerve cord in verticality by maintaining the length and breadth of the primary axis, regardless of its angle to the ground. *Use* of the back should be exactly the same (but not rigid) in standing, sitting, crawling, and any position between.

When the primary axis aligns with the vertical axis, magic happens. Verticality in standing allows whirls, spins, and axial turns. The gaze can rotate almost 180° with a turn of the head. We are unique in our full verticality.*

Our uprightness, however, challenges us to maintain the length of the primary axis. Our vertical spines are now at right angles to the surface of the planet, and our faces, mouths, and sense organs have likewise rotated 90° to keep our direction of orientation toward the horizon. Note that even one degree beyond the perpendicular, however, will put feet or hips in lead so that the bony spinal column may no longer be able to protect the length, shape, and space of the delicate nerve cord and may instead actually threaten its well-being.

To maintain our primary axis in verticality, we must think of lengthening from the sit bones and soles of our feet upwards to the brainstem. This lengthening should be the main event in each and every activity. Let the neural material between the ears get as high as possible while keeping the

A toddler's legs "just tagging along."

---

* Meerkats and leaping dolphins also have acquired these skills, but verticality is not their ongoing modus operandi. Penguins move easily from verticality to swimming.

back in the back. Don't reach with the eyes to see—allow visual images to land on the retinae at the back of the eyeballs.

In the pictures of baseball great Tim Lincecum on the next two pages, his eyes are open and wide with the retinae on the same vertical plane as his sit bones. His back is totally back. His eyes, the highest motor organs connected to the brainstem, are totally receptive.

In other pictures notice how athletes and meerkats and get the very top of their nerve cords and the backs of their eyes up as high as possible. Adopt an erect "listening posture" to let sounds and images come into you.

The head is poised, not positioned.

– Judith Liebowitz

There is no sense of heaviness of the heads of either of these children. Their feet, legs, and whole bodies are recruited to get their eyes up.

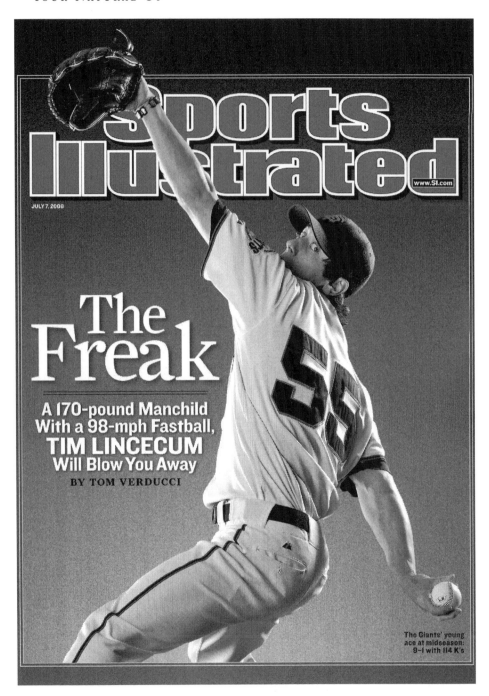

Sports Illustrated

www.SI.com

JULY 7, 2008

The Freak

A 170-pound Manchild With a 98-mph Fastball, TIM LINCECUM Will Blow You Away

BY TOM VERDUCCI

The Giants' young ace at midseason: 9–1 with 114 K's

Tim Lincecum triptych: Note the awareness and aliveness – the organization along the spine all the way up to the back of the eyes on a line with the sit bones.

Roger Federer with his head as upright as possible. Vision is coming into the back of his of eyes. There is a clear vertical line from his sit bones to ears. The plane of the back remains entirely in back.

The plane from back of Michael Vick's eyes to his sit bones defines the unity of the primary axis.

The idea of the *use of the self*

The basic principle of **good use** is to maintain the integrity of the *primary axis*. Head, neck, and spine function together as the whole back, a mainstay that gets strength from its length. *Lengthening* and *widening* should be an ongoing activity for *good use* and well-being. Never shorten, narrow, or diminish your stature.

Head and spine like to come back to center, neutral. Chronic misalignment characterizes **poor use** where, usually, either the head is not leading or the back is shortened by not staying back. Locking one's knees will exaggerate the lumbar curve by pushing it forward.

Haile Selassie

Shay Paulsmeyer and Arthur Rubinstein - The occiput, the back of the head, is just (or almost) as far back as the rest of the back.

Dancers often learn to tuck their tail bones, thereby pushing the lower part of their vertebral columns forward with respect to the rest of their backs. Alexander pulled his head back and down, pushing his cervical spine forward, as in both of the illustrations on this page. Military posture, with shoulders pulled back, *narrows* the back and thrusts the spine forward, decreasing respiratory volume.

Poor use characterizes the teenage slump in its myriad variations. It affects the well-being of the entire organism. Over time, *poor use* takes a toll; it will be elaborated in Chapters 6 and 7. The next chapter proposes an effective method for re–engaging the verticality of your natural up.

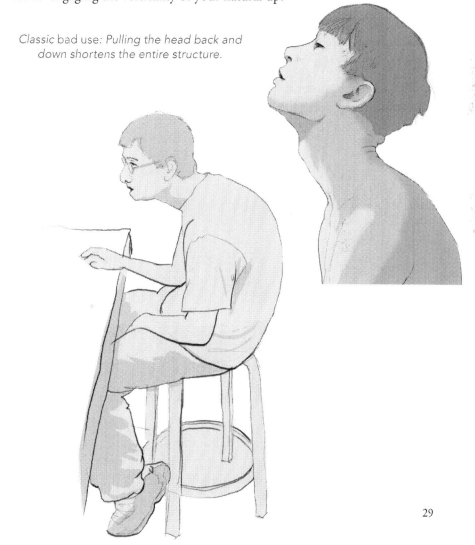

Classic bad use: *Pulling the head back and down shortens the entire structure.*

Good Use

Chief Manuelito

Sri Yukteswar

Somali youth

Prairie dog and Meercats getting their
senses up. Note how they appear to listen
with the back of their eyes?

Bad Use

The Model's Cool

- Back NOT back; leading with hips.
- Pushing the lower back forward.

Military Posture

- Pushing chest out; pushing back forward.
- Narrowing the back between the shoulder blades.
- Decreasing wingspan.

Jeremy Duncan

- Head not leading.
- Knees leading.
- Except for the hump, he is pushing most of his back forward.
- Concave chest.

Entertaining the notion of crawling
will promote the headward orientation necessary for
good use.

CHAPTER 3

Is Crawling an Option?

The previous chapter discussed man's unique evolution to verticality and the potential accompanying problems because of our big heads. This short chapter proposes that (after re-learning to crawl) just *entertaining the notion of crawling* will promote the headward orientation necessary for *good use*. For crawling to be an option, you must be able to organize yourself to crawl with no initiating adjustment.

Our hardwiring dictates that the brainstem leads movement. Crawling exerts the same lengthening influence on the entire body enjoyed by our vertebrate cousins in their horizontal movement. When fish came onto land and evolved into amphibians, their heads continued to lead movement. The limbs, supporting the primary axis off the ground, were just along for the ride.

The amphibian head evolved to be separate from the torso, which created a neck and expanded the head's range of motion. This meant that the leading end of the nerve cord, the brainstem, now resided inside the skull, while the remainder of the nerve cord was re-named the *spinal cord*.

The mechanics of crawling will be detailed in Chapter 6. For now just investigate the crawl position on the four limb pillars that hold the primary axis off the ground. Note the arch that the front limbs make with the upper back,

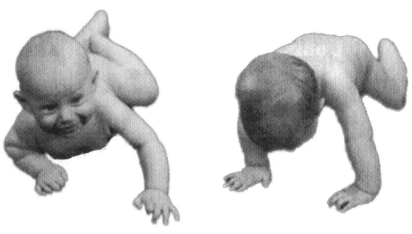

which facilitates *widening*. Let the palms spread with the weight and keep them facing a bit inward.

When you start to move, be curious as to where the senses lead. Imagine the brainstem extending into *doggie eyes* at the crown of your head and let that lead. (Although babies don't crawl this way, it's a good way for adults to start because of our habits of pulling our heads into our torsos.)

Don't let the hands get out in front, but insist that the limbs be recruited to ride on the movement of the primary axis. I make sure my students know how to initiate a crawl from a sitting position; in big groups I ask students to move from walking to crawling to walking again, emulating a toddler's easy, ongoing transitions, while effortlessly following the head.

Alexander's *up* is the direction that lengthens the the spine. If you believe crawling is an option and that the head (the brainstem) is indeed leading, you are "directing upward."

By entertaining the notion of crawling when standing, your body will be light and ready. Engaging your option to crawl connects you through your feet to the ground and brings attention to a "head leading" intentionality.

If you stand without bracing, locking, or overextending, you should be ready to crawl. From standing to sitting or crawling, the angle of the primary axis to gravity will vary moment to moment, but the relationships of its main components stay the same.

Everyone benefits from crawling. Entertaining the notion of crawling will convince upright humans to believe that they do, indeed, follow their heads in movement.

The next two chapters look at the investigation and discoveries of FM Alexander and the technique he developed for psycho-physical re-education.

Even when standing, is crawling an option?

Frederick Matthias Alexander in New York City around 1916

CHAPTER 4

Alexander's Story

Frederick Matthias Alexander was born in Tasmania, Australia in 1869. He was a sickly child who aspired to become a Shakespearian reciter, the pinnacle of entertainment in those days. While still a teenager, however, he started losing his voice while reciting. The doctors had no answers—rest helped, but once he returned to the stage he would lose his voice again. Finally he decided, "It must be something that I am *doing* with myself." For nine years he spent hours in front of a 3-way mirror figuring it out. Very quickly he observed that every time he began to speak he pulled his head back and down toward the shoulder blades. This exaggerated the cervical curve of his spine, shortened his stature, and compressed his larynx, changing the timber and quality of his voice.

Awareness of this habitual action sparked Alexander's process of self-discovery. Likewise, awareness of habit is the first step for people embarking on the journey of improving their own *use*.

Since his habit when beginning to speak was to pull his head "back and down," Alexander decided to put his head *forward and up* the next time. However, even when he *thought* he was putting his head forward and up, he was, in fact, pulling it back and down more than ever. He didn't know and couldn't feel what he was doing with his body. (But he could see it in the mirrors.*) He dubbed this faulty sensory appreciation *debauched kinaesthesia*.

Alexander next noticed that it was not the moment when he began to speak that he pulled his head back and down, but when he decided (or got the stimulus) to speak. He realized that "*the mere thought of an activity was sufficient to enervate the muscles that habitually perform that activity.*"[1] He had to learn to

---

* Because he wasn't actually doing what he thought he was doing, Alexander realized his observations in the mirrors would take constant vigilance.

be able to think about speaking, as well as actually speak, while preventing his habitual reaction of first pulling his head back and down. He eventually called this *refusal to respond* in the habitual manner **inhibition** and he considered it to be the cornerstone of his Technique. *Inhibition*, the pause between stimulus and response, creates the opportunity for choice and change.

With persistence and vigilance, Alexander found he could, to some extent, stop pulling his head back and down, and when he did so, his voice problems improved. He came to understand that the relation of the head to the neck and to the rest of the body constituted a master reflex* of the whole organism. "The way the head is oriented determines the tone and manner of behavior of the whole body."[2]

Eventually Alexander created a set of *directions* for his mind to give to his body to ensure an ongoing ideal relationship of the parts of the body to each other in movement and in rest. Alexander's *directions* go:

> I am going to direct or order my neck† to be free so that my head can move forward and up in such a manner that my whole back can lengthen and widen—widening into my upper arms and sending my knees forward and away—away from the back and slightly away from each other. These directions should be thought "all together, one after the other."

These *directions* are not just orders, but also directions in three-dimensional space. They encourage the whole structure to take up as much space as possible: lengthening, widening, and expanding multi-directionally. They encourage every major joint to move away from every other joint, increasing the volume of the entire organism. The lengthening starts with the back of the head so that the highest joint connecting the head to the neck, the atlanto-occipital (AO) joint, can be spacious.

When Alexander focused on his *directions* instead of his speaking, he could speak without problems. The directions became a *means* that overruled his *end-gaining* to speak.

---

* later dubbed the "primary control."

† When Alexander said *"neck,"* he was primarily concerned with the suboccipital muscles, the small muscles at the nape of the neck that can pull the back of the head toward the first few vertebrae. A good look at the neck, however, shows all sorts of muscles running from the head to low on the torso. *All* of these muscles should be kept free.

The direction of *forward and up* is a point of great confusion in Alexander's work. Because his habit was to tighten his suboccipital muscles, he called that resultant movement *back and down*, and the undoing of it *forward and up*. Most people, however, already carry their heads in front of their torsos and must learn to move their heads and necks *back in space* so that the relationship of head to neck is such that the head *can* fall forward off its point of balance at the top of the spine. The head doesn't actually fall forward, because its weight will be counterbalanced by the tensile pull of the suboccipital muscles. The information of that stretch ripples through the entire structure.*

Alexander's *up* is the direction that lengthens the entire structure to create a lightness that has become a hallmark of the *Alexander Technique*.

Alexander's work began as a search for a cure to his persistent hoarseness and loss of voice. He cured his voice problem, improved his poise and bearing, and inadvertently stumbled on some universal scientific truths. The Alexander Technique is all about NOT DOING anything to undermine the integrity of the back. *Awareness* of habit is the first step; then *inhibition* (not doing); then *direction*. This idea of non-doing is also at the heart of many Eastern philosophies—pay attention, be here now; if you concern yourself with the present (the means), the future (the end) will take care of itself.

Change involves carrying out an activity against the habit of life.

– FM Alexander

Alexander saw that our uprightness could be our undoing. He believed that "man's supreme inheritance"[†] was the ability and need to take conscious control of his own *use*.

For the first ten or fifteen years of his investigations, Alexander considered his work to be about breathing and elocution. In Australia he was dubbed "the Breathing Man." He would say, "it's all about breathing, but don't mention

---

* Tensegrity. See Chapter 7
† The title of Alexander's first book.

the word."* His students improved and word got around; doctors referred new students. These medical recommendations helped him get started in London, where he moved in 1904.

Alexander saw that when people improved their respiration, they improved the *use* of their entire selves. He eventually described his teaching as "one of changing and controlling reaction."[3] "He encouraged his students to work on themselves—at first before going to sleep and upon waking up, but eventually during more and more of their waking hours."[4]

Alexander accepted new students only if they would commit to lessons at least five days a week for the first month or so. This frequency of repeating the kinesthetic experience helped ensure success.

Alexander wrote four books. *Man's Supreme Inheritance (MSI)* was published in 1910 and revised in 1918. *Constructive Conscious Control of the Individual (CCCI)* is a handbook sans pareil for every Alexander teacher. Alexander's third book, *The Use of the Self, published in 1932,* is the shortest and easiest to understand and introduces the concept of *inhibition.* His fourth book is titled *A Universal Constant in Living (UCL).* These books are not easy reading. Paragraph-long sentences present convoluted ideas: ("The inhibitory idea becomes the primary means of the volitionary act," "Belief is a matter of muscular tension," "Debauched kinesthesia" and its consequences, etc.) After his first book he recruited editing assistance.[†]

---

* Breathing is the one autonomic activity with which we can consciously interfere.
† Irene Tasker, Ethel Webb, and later, Walter Carrington.

From 1914 to 1924 Alexander spent half of most years in the United States. Since his first days of teaching his work in Australia he had apprenticed a few other people, but he didn't begin a formal training course until 1931, when he was over 60.* One of his medical champions, Dr. Peter Macdonald, had admonished him: "This is all going to die with you if you are not careful. It's time to start training teachers."[6]

Alexander's discoveries and work could easily not have survived his death in 1955, as

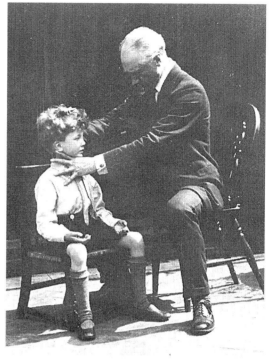

he had resisted† all efforts to establish a society, which might have provided a trademark and set training standards. In his last years and immediately after his death "splinter groups" arose and people with virtually no training posed as teachers. Fortunately Alexander's niece Marjory Barlow and her husband Wilfred had begun their own training course in 1950 and in 1958 spearheaded the formation of STAT, the Society for Teachers of the Alexander Technique, which now sets the standards for international affiliation. (www.stat.org.uk.) www.alexandertechniqueworldwide.com will link you to certified teachers anywhere in the world.

Alexander realized that his doing was his undoing.

– Frank Pierce Jones

---

* He considered the whole idea of a training course to be endgaining.[5]
† When he realized he could be outvoted.[7]

In 1964 American Lulie Westfeldt bragged: "There are more teachers being trained in a competent and responsible manner than ever before."[8] This is equally true today, a half century later.

Alexander began teaching his work to others in 1894 and through the years many notable people took lessons. In the early 1900s scientists* began to verify his findings and eventually contributed to his vocabulary. They found that the leading end of the nervous system, the brainstem, is a *primary control* for the whole body, and that the integrity of the back, the unity of the head with the torso, is paramount to well-being.

Scientists were most impressed with how Alexander, a layman, was able to follow the scientific method during his nine-year investigation in front of the mirror. He tested his hypotheses instead of trying to prove them right and changed them repeatedly before arriving at one that couldn't be proved wrong: inhibiting habitual reactions, especially shortening, and maintaining length, width, and volume.

Validation for Alexander's work came not just from scientists, but from thinkers like Aldous Huxley and George Bernard Shaw. The American educator John Dewey wrote the introduction to three of Alexander's books and opined that "The Alexander Technique bears the same relationship to education that education itself bears to all other human activities."[9] In 1973 Nobel Prize-winning scientist Nikolas Tinbergen devoted half of his acceptance speech to lauding Alexander.

Physiologists have continued to verify his work, studying the "postural set" elicited by the stimulus to act and *inhibition*, that space in time between stimulus and response.† Hundreds of articles on habit and reflex have been published in the last few decades.

Alexander was known for his twinkle, his love of theater, his appreciation for fine food, and his penchant for betting on the horses.

---

* Magnus, Coghill, Sherrington

† *Inhibition* distinguishes the Alexander Technique from all other "mind/body" modalities.

FM Alexander in 1941.

The most valuable knowledge we can possess is of
the use and functioning of the self.
– FM Alexander

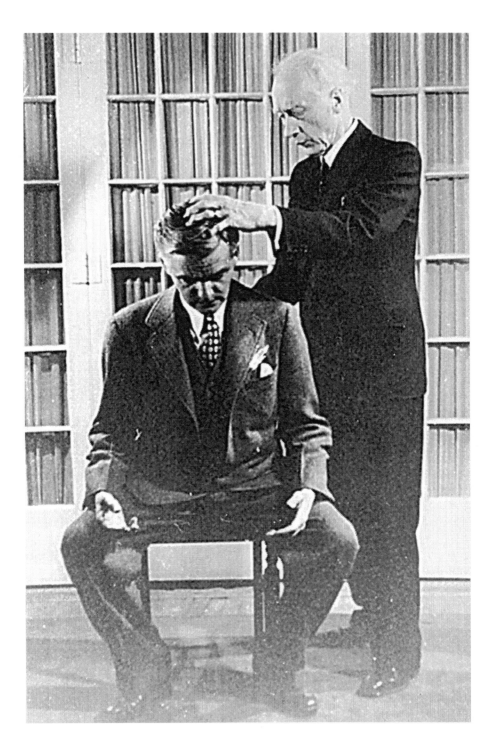

CHAPTER 5

Taking an Alexander Lesson

Alexander lessons begin with an awareness of how you are *using* and *misusing* yourself. Because lifetime habits of *use* tend to feel right and comfortable, anything different will feel awkward, off-balance, and not right. Alexander lessons teach you to short-circuit your habits in order to cultivate a better *use* of yourself.

If your kinesthesia is debauched your habit will feel right, so you can't trust your feelings. You have to be willing to be moved in a way you have never moved before. Embrace not knowing. Alexander said, "It is the trying to be right that will get you wrong."

The AT teacher will take you through everyday activities like sitting, standing, and walking, while preventing you from pulling your head back and down, which would interfere with the integrity of your primary axis. This gives a new kinesthetic experience of the activity, which will develop over time into a new movement habit.

There is often an element of the childhood game, *Mother, May I?*, in an Alexander lesson. Student and teacher will agree upon an activity, but the student doesn't actually *do* the activity until the teacher gives a signal, usually non-verbal, to do so.* This refusal to respond prevents pre-movements that the student's body might feel it needs to do in order to carry out the agreed-upon activity. Be quiet throughout your body. Listen and wait.

Allow yourself to be moved by the teacher while maintaining the integrity of your primary axis. Don't help, but be willing. Alexander lessons involve moving or being moved like a marionette without pulling the head back and down, shortening, or narrowing. Since the student's job is to do nothing, use that time to cultivate awareness, enliven your senses, and think directions of expansion.

---

* Alexander would say: "Now when I tell you to do something, don't do it." Frank Hand in *The Philosopher's Stone* p.39.

Good use is not about holding a posture or straightening the spine. Both create a robot-like (*Alexandroid*) posture, which is liable to lead to pinched nerves. The Alexander Technique advocates neither exaggerating the curves of the spine nor shortening the primary axis in any manner. When you quit pulling your head back and down, it may feel like you are tucking your chin, but that's not what's really happening. Your angle of sight to the horizon may lower, but the eyelids will know to respond by opening more.

In Alexander jargon, "back and down" vs "forward and up" can be confusing. To repeat from the previous chapter: most people have to let their whole head and neck move back and up in space so that the poised head at the top of the neck/back *can* fall forward off its point of balance at the top of the spine to exert a tensile pull on the suboccipital muscles. Alexander teacher Bruce Fertman calls it "that forward undertow movement that collects the whole body upward."[1]

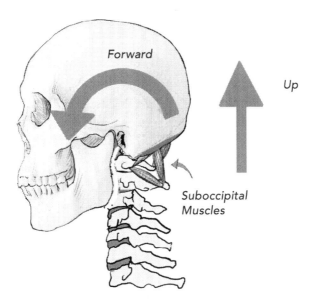

Forward *is a point of confusion for people learning about the Alexander Technique, since most people already carry their heads in front of their torsos. Forward refers to the forward pivot of the head at the top of the spine, as the weight of the jaw makes the skull slightly heavier in front of the pivot point. (The face does not fall downward, nor is the chin tucked.)*

Up *refers to the direction that lengthens the spine.*

Alexander said, "You are not here to do exercises or to learn to do something right, but to learn to meet a stimulus that always puts you wrong and to learn to deal with it. Stop the things that are wrong first." For most of us the stimulus to sit in a chair (or just thinking about sitting) will trigger an habitual "postural set." Alexander scholar Frank Pierce Jones said that he was unable to move at all without first tensing in his habitual manner:

> Further light was shed on my use of myself in activity when Alexander, a second time, altered the relationship of my head and neck to the rest of my body, and then asked me to move without changing what he had done. When I realized the full implication of what was being asked of me, I became glued to the spot. My feelings told me that unless I made some preliminary changes movement was not possible. As a preliminary to any movement I felt compelled to increase the tension in my neck and draw my head closer to my body until it occupied a position that felt 'natural.'[2]

Because we are hardwired for the head to go first in movement, we MUST honor that orientation, even though a horizontal direction of locomotion is no longer automatically reinforcing the lengthening of our now vertical spines. Our sense organs and mouth have also rotated 90° from the direction that lengthens the spine, so we must *direct up* to maintain length, strength, and space in the primary axis.

Your feet should touch the floor as delicately as your head moves forward and up.

– Marj Barstow

Before beginning a lesson review the weight-bearing points of the body to reinforce your sense of contact with the ground. Each foot offers a tripod of support; in sitting the sit bones support the primary axis. The flex of the knees should go over the first two toes. *Entertain the notion of crawling* from both standing and sitting upright in a chair.

Alexander's Procedures

Alexander developed a series of procedures* which most teachers use as a foundation for their work. They are simple and don't take up a lot of space. The chair is both a prop for the activities of sitting to standing and a stimulus, challenging the student's tendency to *end-gain* for that seat. The upright chair has become a symbol of Alexander's work.

An Alexander lesson usually includes chair work, a table lesson ("lying-down work") and a bit of walking. Getting in and out of a chair is a perfect activity for learning not to shorten the primary axis in activity. Sitting on a chair, you will walk your sit bones forward to the edge of the chair to eliminate the extra sensory information coming in through the back of your legs. Many people notice that the moment their sit bones touch the chair's surface, their bodies collapse into that contact and abandon any headward orientation. The chair can be any height. The torso, from the sit bones to the ears, should retain its length and shape, while the leg joints bend and extend.

You will probably begin by standing in front of the chair not knowing what's going to happen next. (Will you sit? Go up on your toes? Take a short walk? Crawl?) While standing in a non-habitual manner, you may feel like you're going to fall over; you may have more weight on the heels than you are accustomed.

The Alexander teacher will help you maintain your head/neck/back relationship, while you do (or don't do) the agreed-upon activity.

During early chair lessons, keeping the entire surface area of the foot in contact with the floor is often very difficult. Note how you may undermine your own support by unweighting a portion of the foot—scrunching your toes or rolling to the outside of the foot. Find and trust the contact of the foot with the floor!

---

* Presented in detail in the next chapter.

Taking an Alexander lesson

Chair work teaches you to stop *end-gaining* to sit or stand. Instead pay attention to the *means-whereby* by following your head and maintaining the length of the torso. This repeated kinesthetic experience is the "rote learning" of Alexander's work; it reinforces new neuromuscular pathways.

In getting in or out of a chair you will pass through **monkey**, a *position of mechanical advantage* that increases stability by lowering one's center of gravity. It is the crouched ready-position of athletes and guitar players.

In the lying-down lesson, you will lie on your back in the *semi-supine position* on a table or the floor with the

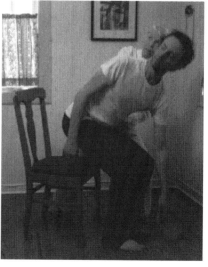

flat surface informing you about the plane of your back. Because you are safe, you can release all unnecessary muscular tension. You'll probably be asked to keep your eyes open. Find the thirteen points of bony contact listed in the next chapter.

Your teacher will move your head and limbs one by one. Let her. Trust the teacher's hands, allowing that contact to reassure your sense of support, so that your muscles can continue to release. The whole body is connected. There are many things to inhibit, so the more you can trust the contact with the teacher and table, the easier it will be to stop holding. Think: "Let, let, allow."

For many students Alexander's work will awaken the upper back, the thoracic spine, giving power to that area so dominant in the newborn.

Purportedly Alexander said it would take 25-30 lessons to make a lasting change in one's *use*. Even one lesson, however, is a big start, since awareness of one's habits of *use* is such a big first step. Most teachers now give 30-45 minute lessons and ask that you initially come weekly or even twice a week. Frequent repetition reinforces the new kinesthetic experience of better *use*. Ultimately students must engage their own awareness and thinking to learn to inhibit and direct. The Alexander Technique stresses *not diminishing your stature*. It is NOT about straightening the spine, which needs those curves.

When moving from sitting to standing, or vice versa, follow your head. Trust the contact of the soles of your feet with the floor and believe that crawling is an option. Ask: "What is my contact with the ground? Do I trust that contact? Am I moving up off it? Is crawling an option?"

Find the feet, follow the head.

– Cathy Pollock

What happens in an AT lesson? You re-educate your kinesthetic sense to improve the reliability of sensory feedback. Physiological benefits include: "Appearing taller, more balanced with less muscular effort. Movement is smoother, more efficient. Voice production and respiration improve."[3] Alexander called his work "psychophysical re-education."

Change takes time and your muscles and connective tissue won't necessarily be happy about it. Says Louise Morgan in her diary of a friend's lessons with Alexander in the early 1950s:

> The new aches and pains still go on. But Alexander has no pity on me. He says "Splendid!" when I tell him I ache all over. He even tells me he is glad to hear that I'm stiffer and achier and sorer—that means good things are happening to me. The old muscle pattern is changing. No—I am changing my muscle pattern![4]

Note how she takes credit for the change, for what she is *doing* with herself. There is a story about a young girl with scoliosis taking lessons with Alexander. After her first lesson she complained to her mother that he had "put me all crooked." That was the girl's debauched kinesthesia—her curved spine felt right, while diminishing the curvature felt the opposite of what it was.

Experience different teachers. Their words, hands, procedures, and perspectives will differ while the essence of their message remains the same. Give it time; the process of changing lifetime habits takes time.

Maintaining the integrity of the primary axis doesn't preclude spirals. An Alexander lesson might include rotating around the primary axis—turning to look at the ceiling, while rising from a chair or going into *monkey*, as seen in the two photographs on page 51.

The starting point of the Alexander Technique
is stopping, doing nothing.

– Glen Park

Personal Notes

I hadn't been warned about the dangers of trying to be right. After my first Alexander workshop I came home thinking the AT was all about straightening my neck and became an "Alexandroid" until excruciating pain down my right arm sent me to a chiropractor. My attempt at straightening my neck squashed the discs and pinched nerves—I'm lucky I didn't do permanent damage.

During my three years of training to become a teacher my whole body expanded, a common occurrence. I outgrew my wardrobe, with blouses now two inches too narrow on each shoulder and three inches too small around the ribs. (More than once Alexander admonished men who were embarking upon a series of lessons not to invest in a new suit just yet.)

Expanding the body, allowing every joint to move away from every other joint, creates more room for fat to spread and therefore a leaner look. In the mid-1960s a *Harper's Bazaar* article about the Alexander Technique, "Take Inches Off Your Waistline," electrified the country and produced far more requests for lessons than the small number of AT teachers in the US at that time could accommodate.*

I spent a dozen years in an office holding the telephone's receiver between my left ear and shoulder, freeing my right hand to write. That postural habit eventually felt right and can be seen in the photo of me with my mentors on page 130.

I have seen people develop arches in their feet as they began to trust the tripods of contact with the ground. I learned I was becoming a good teacher when my students progressed during hiatuses in lessons. At least two of my students have themselves become teachers.

Awareness, inhibition, and direction are the three principles of the Alexander Technique. Can we learn *not to do* our bad habits of *use* and movement? Can we move into and out of *positions of mechanical advantage* without shortening the primary axis? Without pulling the head back and down? *Is crawling an option?* Can you regain *your natural up?*

---

* The American Center for the Alexander Technique (ACAT) kept a list—as newly trained teachers moved to the west coast, they immediately had full teaching practices.

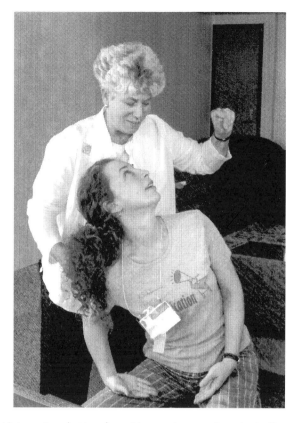

Using visual stimulus, Alexander teacher Judy Stern coaxes colleague Eileen Troberman into a spiral.

There are 26 bones in the foot, or maybe 27, and they're all moving away from each other.*

– Frank Ottiwell

---

* Extrapolating: There are 206 bones in the body and they're all moving away from each other.

St. Louis Cardinal Ozzie Smith does his famous backflip during the 1985 World Series. Notice that his back and head are on the same plane.

CHAPTER 6

The Use of The Self

The *Use of The Self* is the title of Alexander's third book. How you *use* yourself affects how you function and, over time, how you are structured. "Alexander realized that the choices we make about what we *do* with ourselves to a large extent determine the quality of our lives."[1]

This chapter presents various modes of moving and being in space that are anatomically beneficial and biomechanically efficient. Alexander taught that these *positions of mechanical advantage* fostered *good use*.

Lengthening the primary axis should be the main event in each and every activity. The universal themes in all movement should be to *inhibit* shortening and to *direct* expansion; relax, but don't collapse; head leads and body follows; keep the brainpan up. Trust your contact with the ground and the support that contact provides. To maintain the *integrity of the primary axis*, the back and head should stay in line.

Organizing yourself to crawl can insure that you are leading with your head— it is a shortcut to good *use*. Marj Barstow said, "If you're *directing*, you *are* inhibiting." If crawling is indeed a movement option, you *are* directing.

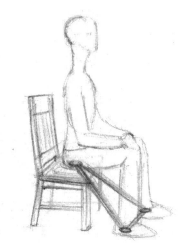

The Sitting Tripod

The *sit bones* are well-designed rockers that support the primary axis in sitting. When sitting in a chair, find the tripod* of support: two feet and the sit bones. Send the knees over the toes.

When sitting on the *edge of the chair,* maintain the integrity of the primary axis while rocking back and forth on the sit bones. Notice more weight on the feet as you hinge forward. Are you able to hinge without tightening your neck? Can you feel the sit bones roll? Can you feel the change in angle of the sit bones in relationship to the chair? Can you tell whether the angle of the crest of the hipbone to the thigh is closing? Does the entire surface of the sole of each foot maintain contact with the floor? Is crawling an option?

Before moving on, investigate also the primary axis in a cone of movement from the base of the sit bones.

There are many other ways of sitting, as illustrated at the beginning of Chapters 2 and 3, for instance.

The sitting cone

---

* Since the two sit bones are 3-4 inches apart, the sitting tripod is actually a "sitting trapezoid." However, the tripod idea works perfectly for involving the feet and actually using the sit bones while sitting in a flat-bottomed chair.

Standing

Your vertical axis extends from the soles of the feet to the top of your head. Find that opposition. What is your contact with the ground? Do you trust it? Are you moving headward up off it? In standing, the tripods of the feet are your contact with the ground, conducting upthrust toward the headtop.

Be light and easy in ankle and knee joints. If you can wiggle the toes without moving your axis you are balanced and not "holding yourself up." Let the knees be soft—you should be able to delicately move them back and forth without actually bending them or moving your axis.

The back, defining the primary axis, should remain in back. The sit bones dangle behind the knees, pointing away from the headtop. Crawling should always be an option, creating a *hint of monkey* even in perfect uprightness.

Just as with sitting, you should be able to find a cone of movement with your standing vertical axis. With feet together, imagine a laser beam pointing upward from your headtop inscribing a circle on the ceiling while allowing your weight to travel around the perimeters of your feet.

Notice the possibilities, the magic, of being vertical. Sense organs are as high as possible, allowing 360° of awareness with a turn of the head. When the primary axis of the body is vertical, it aligns with gravity, creating the possibility of spins, spirals, and the generation of centrifugal and centripetal forces.

In preparation for walking, try this exercise: Stand with feet 3-4 inches apart, weight divided evenly. Keep the weight 50/50 while raising one heel to bring that foot up onto its ball, then back to its full tripod without shifting your hips to one side or changing the shape of your primary axis.

Walking

Now take this exercise into walking backward with minimal shift of your axis. Notice how walking backward helps to collect your whole body back and up into the back.

Continue organizing yourself to walk backward, but instead walk forward by letting your knee swing forward from the hip until the heel makes contact with the floor. Transfer your weight, rolling through the tripod then ball of the foot, as you allow the rear foot to unweight and then swing forward.

When you walk, the feet alternate in bearing weight. If you can allow the natural *contralateral* movement of the spiraling torso to bring the opposite arm forward, you will maintain an upward/headward directionality without lurching from side to side. This contralateral movement is equally important for smooth running.

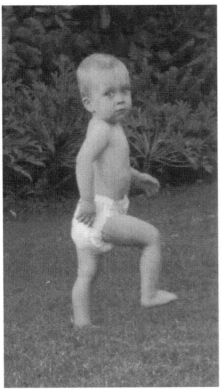

Verticality and bipedality are not synonymous. The latter, locomotion on two legs, happens with a few other animals—most birds and some reptiles like t-rex. Our legs in the bipedal gait are a bit like pendulums and a bit like spokes.

I really think I prefer "going up" to "pulling down."

– Walter Carrington

Anton's contralateral

Tennis greats Chris Evert and Steffi Graff maintain the plane of their backs in monkey.

Monkey

Monkey* is a folded posture anywhere between standing and squatting with all six leg joints (hips, knees, ankles) flexed. It lowers one's center of gravity and increases stability, while maintaining the integrity of the primary axis. We use this *position of mechanical advantage* constantly and see it everywhere. Can you move in and out of *monkey* without shortening your primary axis or pulling your head back and down?

Look at the sketches in this chapter of athletes, children, musicians, and normal people. The leg joints bend while the primary axis maintains its length and width. *Monkey* is a key to power and connection.

---

* Dubbed thus by the students in Alexander's first teacher training class.

Baseball player and lemuriformes. The eyes lead the structure into length. Note the line from the back of the eyes to the sit bones.

*Golfer Adam Scott addressing the ball. Check out the integrity of his primary axis in his **monkey**.*

Baseball batter

Aim up and stay back
under all conditions.

– Patrick Macdonald

Andre Agassi's eyes are so receptive! His back is back, his primary axis is lengthening from the sit bones to the back of the eyes.

The crown of Charles Barkley's head leads and his body follows. His back is back and his peripheral awareness comes from the back of his eyes. Notice the push and spring from the sole of his left foot.

The artist Prince staying up while "getting down."

*Alexander and Marjean in lunge while giving Alexander lessons.
That's artist Christopher Neville with Marjean.*

Lunge

Lunge, standing with one foot in front and at an angle to the other, is a slight variation of either standing or *monkey* depending on the bend of the knees and the distance between the feet. Weight can be shifted from mostly on one foot or the other. The angle of the torso can vary in both tilt and turn and can change its orientation with a pivot of the feet. Stable and resistant, this position of mechanical advantage is used in taiji and fencing and is famous as the Suzuki violin stance. It is used frequently by Alexander teachers, as illustrated in the above photos of Alexander and Marjean giving lessons.

Squatting African woman holding child and receiving ritual bathing.

Squat

The squat = standing folded.[2] It's common in toddlers and people of all ages in chairless societies. Note that the heels stay connected with the ground.

To practice this without lifting your heels, put a few inches of books under the heels—over time your Achilles tendons will lengthen so you can gradually decrease the book height.

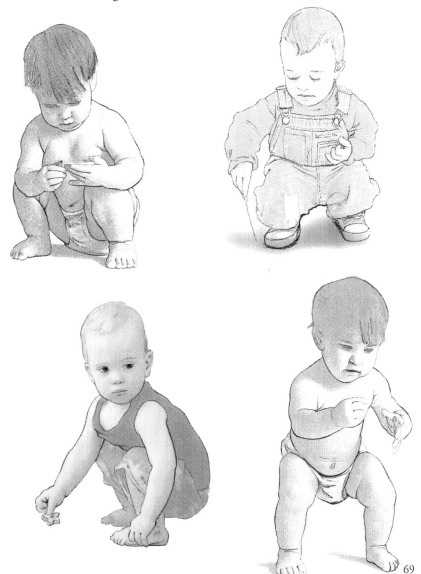

Crawling

Re-read chapter 3, which introduces the crawl position and the essentials of locomotion on all-4's. Let crawling define the head-leading aspect of your primary axis to emulate tetrapod locomotion. Most people should soften the floor with a carpet or rug.

Crawling from the sitting tripod

In the sitting tripod your points of contact are the tripods of the feet and the two sit bone rockers. Trust the contact of these weight-bearing surfaces so that you can move away from them, following the head to lengthen the segmented structure. Send the knees over the first two toes.

In the chair, following the head and entertaining the notion of crawling, first hinge the primary axis forward. As you hinge forward, the weight goes first to the feet. Try hanging out as shown in the third drawing of the series below. You may not feel the sit bones anymore, but you will definitely feel the weight on your feet.

Now continue following your head into a crawl. At some point your hands will be recruited for support. Allow the balls of the feet to flex as the contact rolls through them, softening the knees' landing on the floor. Ideally the knees will land on a gait, one a little before the other, but don't expect that to happen the first few times. Keep the headward intentionality.

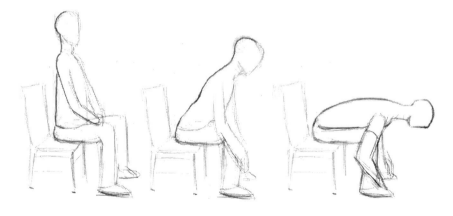

Hinging on the sit bone rockers

Hanging out, folded, with weight on back of thighs and feet, head directing forward, and imaginary senses at head-top.

Following the crown: When ready to crawl, pretend sniffing and investigating from the crown of the head. (Headward intentionality.) Let hands/arms be recruited.

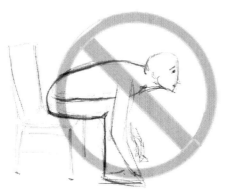

Don't try to look where you're going. Keep the "doggie eyes" at the crown of your head pointed in the direction that lengthens the torso.

Let the crown of your head lead you into horizontal movement. Don't let your hands get ahead of the shoulders.

Refuse to tighten your neck at each and every moment. In time you may look up from a crawl without tightening your neck, but don't try it yet—babies are adept at this, but you probably won't be. Because our eyes have rotated 90° from the direction that lengthens our segmented structures, put imaginary *"doggie eyes"* at the top of your head to lead the crawl. Allow sensory curiosity to lead the body into movement. Pretend to look, sniff, and listen from imaginary senses at the brainstem or the crown of your head.

Continue to acknowledge your contact with the floor and trust its support.

Once you start bearing weight with the palms, you want them to be slightly "pigeon fingered," so that the little fingers are parallel. In the baby's earliest crawl the hands are spread and almost turned in. Allow upthrust through the arms and palms as in the crawl position introduced in Chapter 3.

Moving forward, the hands should articulate, as the feet articulate in walking. Don't shuffle. Again, hands should not get ahead of the torso, as they are only "tagging along." Ditto for the tiny insignificant legs.

The back, the whole back including the occiput (the back of the head) and the neck, should stay in the back, now on top, and not sag. Headward intentionality thwarts the sag. Point the sit bones in a direction opposite the headtop.

Try variations on the classic crawl position by letting the forearms join the palms to participate in bearing weight. Experiment with more or less bend in the knees. Try activating the toes, inviting them to be curious about pushing potential.

Crawling from a chair is something almost anyone, no matter how uncomfortable or frightened, can do. It gets easier after a couple of times. To reassure yourself that you'll be able to get up from the floor, first read the following instructions.

Crawling to standing

To get up from the floor, picture toddlers who use chairs, coffee tables, or walls to assist them in standing. Crawl toward a chair. First put one palm onto the seat of the chair, while the other three limbs remain in crawl position. Then put the second palm onto the seat, so that both forelimbs are again in a crawl position, but higher. Now, trusting your weight to the palms and the one knee remaining on the floor, place the opposite foot flat on the floor. Stand on that foot, using the two palms for balance, in order to bring the second foot flat on the floor parallel to the first. Acknowledge the contact and support of both feet and roll up to vertical.

Using a stable surface (chair, table, or wall) to support your upper body in order to get your feet under you to rise from a crawl.

A second way to rise from a crawl position is to tuck your toes under then walk your hands back to the knees. Putting weight on the palms and keeping your knees softly bent, let your buttocks rise, while your heels drop until they touch the floor. Now allow your palms to walk backward to the feet. Find your feet, and roll up to standing.

Tucking toes under to back up over feet in order to rise from a crawl.

Semi-supine

Semi-supine* is an important *position of mechanical advantage* that reinforces your sense of the plane of your back. It offers practice at doing nothing but giving weight through the contacting surfaces of the head, back, and feet.

Lie supine on the floor[†] with the knees up and feet flat on the floor. Consider placing a book or two under your head. A rough guide for book height is to have the face parallel with ceiling—forehead slightly higher than chin, so that the sub-occipital muscles will be delicately stretched. As your *use* improves, the book height can be lowered.

Semi-supine position has 13 points of bony contact:
>   **Tripods of both feet = 6**
>   **Back of hips, shoulders, elbows on both sides = 6**
>   **Back of head = 1**

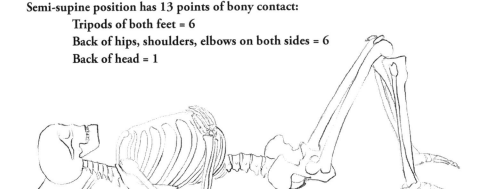

Note the triangle of each knee up and away from the support at back and the soles of the feet. Do nothing but give weight to the floor.

Because you can't fall off the floor, semi-supine facilitates *non-doing* and honors the plane of the back. (If your knees don't want to stay up, just think of a *pelvic tilt.*) Allow the weight of bones, muscle, and innards to fall toward the floor. Allow the *surface area of contact* between you and the floor to increase as you let go of tension and holding. Let the floor give feedback about the plane of your back. In semi-supine you are totally supported by thirteen points of bony contact.

---

* officially, "supine with flexed knees."
† Most people will want to soften the floor by lying on a carpet, rug, blanket, or yoga mat.

Bonobo in semi-supine.

In semi-supine, enjoy the benefits of finding length and width. The horizontal spine is not weight-bearing, so lessening the curves of the spine is not a danger. While in this safe position, allow each vertebral spool to be heavy and to fall planetward by releasing all unnecessarily engaged muscles.

Note the relationship of the leg to the back (page 91). While the teacher moves your leg, the only thing happening at the back is that the short *neck of the femur is being rotated around its own axis*—there is no torque at the hip joint.

In semi-supine just the thought of a pelvic tilt gets the knees to stay up.

When you take the time to lie down, the spongy discs between the vertebrae absorb bodily fluids to become slightly bigger and more taut, thereby creating a little more space between each and every vertebra and a little more length along the entire vertebral structure. (We are taller in the morning than we are at night.) When we increase length, we increase volume, something our entire organism appreciates. Research documents the loss of height during waking hours and the benefits of brief (10 minute) periods of lying down to rejuvenate the discs.*

Note that the relationships of the parts of the body to each other in semi-supine are almost exactly the same as in *monkey*. The primary axis doesn't change. Rotate the pictures of the athletes in *monkey* 90° to see it. (Only the ankle joint is different.)

The relationship of the parts of the body to each other is the same in semi-supine and monkey.

Most Alexander teachers would have their students cultivate the *semi-supine habit*, the practice of lying down once during the middle of every day—lengthening, widening, and directing. Alexander's lying-down work allows time for just noticing, like a newborn, whose only choice is to give weight to the supporting surface.

In Alexander lore there were people who could never manage regular lessons, but still made big improvements in their *use* by regularly "doing their lying-down work."

---

* "Explained by the dehydration of the intervertebral discs due to the effect of gravity on the upright person."[3]

Hurdler demonstrates fantastic head/neck/back relationship.
Her back is clearly in the back!

Misuse: Positions of Mechanical Disadvantage

We don't see *misuse* much in nature. Nor in toddlers. We have to ask: "How do we get this way?" Bad backs seem to be a hallmark of civilization. What happens? Look on the facing page at two 2015 covers of *The New Yorker* magazine that illustrate *good and bad use* while using a portable digital gadget.

Regard the classic photo below, whose caption in Michael Gelb's *Body Learning* reads: "The three gangly youths on the left stand in sharp contrast to the alert child on the right *whose Use of himself has yet to be corrupted.*"[4] Peers clearly play a role in the teenage slump.

People develop habits of *bad use (poor use, misuse)* for many reasons, including emotional and physical trauma and the desire to cultivate some physical ideal. David Gorman says:

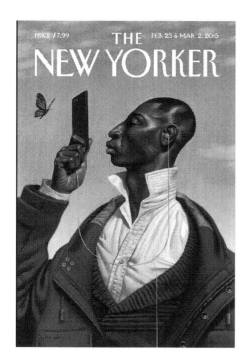

"If we try to hold on to "well-aligned balance," we will be allowing less and less flexibility until we get into a position where we hardly move at all. We are no longer poised, we are postured. At some point the range of deviation becomes so small that it is smaller than the range of flexibility needed for free breathing—we hold onto our breathing so it doesn't disturb our free balance."[5]

Notice habits that diminish your stature. Any kind of *doing* can upset the inherent wisdom of the body. It isn't possible to "do" *good use*—it will happen by itself when you quit interfering.

Trying to be a certain size by sucking in the stomach will create tension throughout the body. "It is as if each of us is trying to take up the least possible amount of room in the universe."[6] Less volume means less space for muscles and fat to spread out. This counterproductively creates more possibilities for bulges and bellies. Less volume also increases blood pressure and constricts internal organs. Pulling-in joint surfaces leads to arthritic conditions. Our bodies work best when they take up as much space as possible. Think geodesically; think of every joint moving away from every other joint.

Charlie Brown tells Sally that he can't be depressed without assuming the appropriate posture.

Parents should not pressure their children to walk too soon. Children first should master the infantile activities of wriggling, rolling, creeping, and crawling that sufficiently strengthen the deep spinal muscles for uprightness. Parents should encourage their infants to find the push from the soles of the feet.

Habits of undermining one's support or not trusting that support will lead to the creation of alternative support through muscular tension. This initiates a cascade of compensatory muscular tensions. Similarly, a lack of emotional or psychological support encourages chronic muscular tension, which diminishes stature and demands compensatory tension. Shyness will create a body language that eventually becomes structure. A person's sense of being awkward will tend to make him so.

Poor use can spiral downwards. "As 'the elderly' begin to experience a loss of confidence in their mobility, they suffer a loss of mobility, which in turn leads to further loss of confidence."[7]

A person gets old because he bends over.

—John Dewey

Listed below are contributors to *poor use*. Possible solutions are suggested in Chapter 8 on lifetime habits.

- The *startle pattern*, associated with anxiety and fear, is a stereotypical response to a loud noise. It changes the head's poise and initiates a wave-like contraction through the body, which mirrors the changes you find in sickness, old age, and lack of exercise.

- Infants skipping developmental stages. Premature walking.

- Imitating *poor use* (usually of a parent or peer).

- Worry. Being worried about not being perfect.

- School children trying to get it right.

- Peer group pressure (teenage slouch).

- Physical or emotional trauma internalized in musculature and structure and now chronic.

Schoolboy slouching over a desk.

- Stresses of modern society.

- Deep couches and easy chairs.

- Car seats and headrests.

- Computers.

- Electronic devices—*texting neck.*

- Ballet dancer's turnout done 24/7.

Gabby slouches on the couch.

*Upper back not back,
hunched forward.*

*Leading with feet.
Holding shoulders up.*

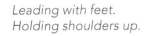

*Leading with face.
Upper back not back.*

*Pushing back forward.
Leading with breasts.*

*Leading with feet.
Tilted back beyond the perpendicular.*

Alexander realized that the choices we make about
what we do with ourselves to a large extent determine
the quality of our lives.

– Michael Gelb

A good slouch.
No sense of sit bones; no plane of back.
Feet are not participating in a sitting tripod to
support the primary axis.

"Military posture"
Pushing chest out and whole back forward.
Sitting on thighs or front of sit bones.

Not using feet to support the primary axis
in a sitting tripod.
Pulling head back and down.
Primary axis clearly compromised.

Sitting on tail bone instead of sit bones.
Back curved forward.
Pulling head back and down to bring brainpan to level.

Sitting on tailbone and slumped downward.
Primary axis clearly compromised.

CHAPTER 7

Tensegrity

BONES   CONNECTIVE TISSUE   REFLEXES

This chapter presents details of human anatomy through the unifying principle of tensegrity.* Most of us have been taught that balance and good posture require the body's weight to be stacked around a central axis, which would restrict range of movement and ask the muscles to work constantly to maintain the central alignment. Fortunately, that's not how our bodies work.

This drawing of a simple tensegrity structure shows how bones can "float in a sea of continuous tension."[2] Notice that the two upper struts are *suspended from below* by elastic tension.

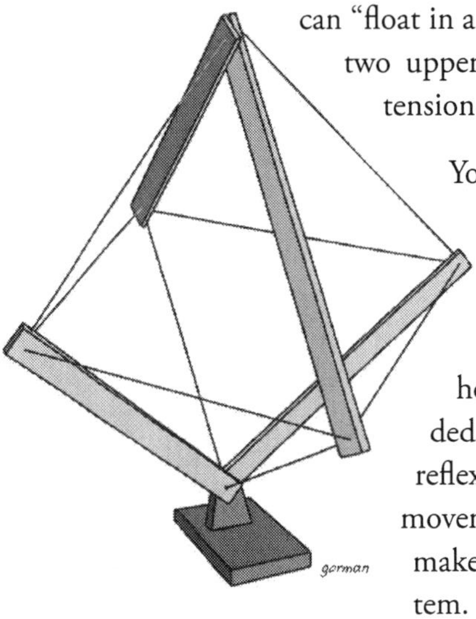

Your body is a living *tensegrity* structure with all parts interrelated in a web of connections. Bones, suspended by muscle and connective tissue in elastic tension, maintain space. Muscles and connective tissue hold the bones in place. Nerve sensors embedded in these tissues send feedback to the brain; reflexes to and from the brain adjust tension and movement in response to those sensory inputs to make a whole, balanced, light and resilient system.

This tensegrity structure shows the weight of the two upper struts suspended by the elastic members below them.

---

* The term tensegrity was coined from "tension integrity" by the designer Buckminster Fuller. (Integrity implies wholeness and completeness.) Tensegrity refers to structures that maintain their integrity due primarily to a balance of continuous tensile forces through the structure.[1]

Fascia is the tensile connective tissue that holds everything together. It is a single net that grows embryonically to surround every muscle, organ, vessel, and structure. It is tacked down in places, but a pull in one place will be felt throughout. (This is why injuries can manifest at a distance from the source of a strain, like a snag in a sweater.)

Fascia is plastic and over time can be stretched. However, it tends to shrink up to the edges of a muscle's range of motion until it feels a stretch. This is a passive protective strategy. "The connective tissue will always tighten up to the borders of your *use*, giving you the range within which you have the skill to operate, while securing you from any potentially damaging excursions beyond."[3]

Fascia is a living, responsive matrix, rich in sensory input. "It reacts and remembers."[4] It surrounds muscle, which can actively change shape, so "over time fascial structure will accommodate posture, locking it in."[5]

Both muscle and fascia pull inward against the outward push of the bones. "Without the soft tissues the bones would clatter to the floor."[6]

THE BONES

Bones are the spacers, *holding shape and maintaining volume.* (Everything inside your container works better with more room.) Because we tend to move according to how we think the bones are shaped and articulate, the main bones of the vertical axis are presented here in some detail.

The bones conduct upthrust through contact with the ground. The ***main beam**** of the primary axis includes the *head, spine, and hip.* Lengthening the main beam should be the "true and primary movement in every act."[7]

The head is the lead bone, containing sense organs and the in-charge neural center at the brainstem. The back of the head, serviced by nerves from the top of the neck, is the head of the back. The head poises on the top of the spine, its weight in front counterbalanced by the elastic suboccipital muscles at the nape of the neck. Our sense organs ("teleceptors") want to be as high as possible, while the *brainpan*, the plane of the base of the skull, likes to be level.

---

* Architecturally "main beam" refers to a horizontal support, which is how the vertebrate back began.

85

The brainpan likes to be level.

The back (including head and hip) defines the primary axis and preserves volume. It encases that all-important *dorsal nerve cord*, whose primacy is no longer self-evident.

The master joint between head and spine, **the atlanto-occipital (AO) joint,** is a *primary control* for the whole body. Sensors imbedded in the muscles and ligaments that span that joint inform the vestibular system about the balance of the head and monitor reflexes of the entire body, tying overall function to the relationship of the head to the neck. The *proprioception,* the sense of the relationship of the parts of the body to each other, of the atlanto-occipital joint is elusive. It is higher up and further back than we think—at the ears just below the thin floor of the skull.*

You may want to review the drawings of the AO joint that were presented in the second chapter: the three views of the the hole at the base of the skull through which the nerve cord passes (p.20); the skull, showing a schematic of the nerve cord (brainstem + spinal cord on p.18); and another skull, showing the suboccipital muscles and the "forward and up" of Alexander directions (p.21).

---

* A good image to give you a sense of the location of the AO joint is: put an imaginary rod through the holes in your ears; let the nod of the head be up and over that rod.

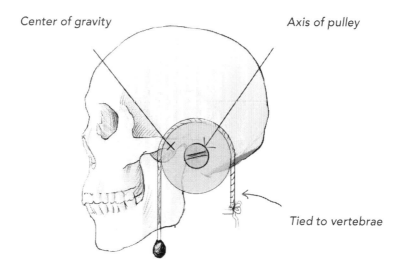

Center of gravity   Axis of pulley

Tied to vertebrae

Pulley image: If allowed, the head is always falling forward off its point of balance.

Here's another view—the *pulley image*. The center of gravity of the head is slightly in front of its point of balance at the AO joint. That weight provides a constant potential energy that "plucks up the back" to suspend the body from the head. This creates the lightness that is a hallmark of the Alexander Technique.

The suboccipital muscles at the nape of the neck should be allowed to stretch delicately to counterbalance the weight of the head. The relationship of the head to the neck/back at the AO joint should be such that the head *can* fall forward from that point of balance, exerting a lengthening influence on the whole segmented structure.

Pulling the head back and down, however, will render the head a dead weight, squashing the body and short-circuiting the tensile feedback of the nerve sensors, interrupting our finely tuned anti-gravity feedback mechanism.

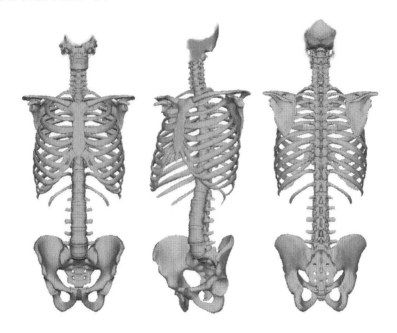

The whole back from three angles.
In function, the back extends from the sit bones to the occiput.
Note the four curves of the spine in the 3/4 view.

The spine is a series of flexible *distortion joints*[8] cushioned by intervertebral discs. Any movement changes the whole segmented structure, which, after moving, wants to return to its original shape that preserves maximum volume for the container.

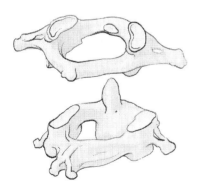

The vertebrae are thick, heavy, and can be imaged as a chain of spools. The top two vertebrae, the *atlas* and *axis*, are specialized to give the head its huge range of motion. (The nodding of the head happens at the AO joint, while turning occurs between the atlas and axis.)

The specialized top two vertebrae, the atlas on top, and the axis below.

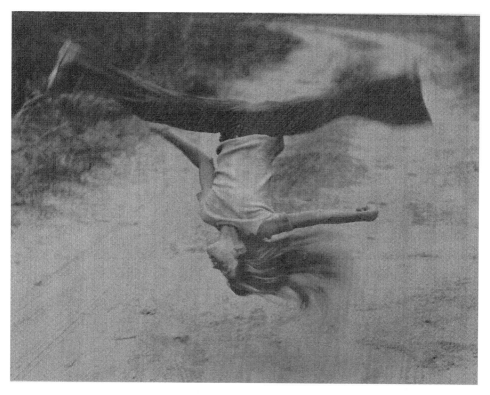

Payson's Aerial by Susie Fitzhugh. Note her prominent sit bones (pointing sky-ward) that define the bottom of her primary axis.

The discs of the spine are elastic and flexible, distorting to accommodate movement of the vertebrae. The discs are remnants of the ancestral notochord and retain its spacer function. When the spine is horizontal, lying down, the discs soak up bodily fluids, creating a bit more space between each and every vertebra. This is why most Alexander teachers would have their students cultivate the "semi-supine habit."

The spine has spring; it is not just a compressed column. Four curves stabilize its segmented verticality. Problems begin when you exaggerate or straighten the spine's curves. Because bipedal upright locomotion doesn't promote lengthening like that enjoyed by our horizontally-moving four-legged cousins, you must constantly remind yourself of that headward directionality.

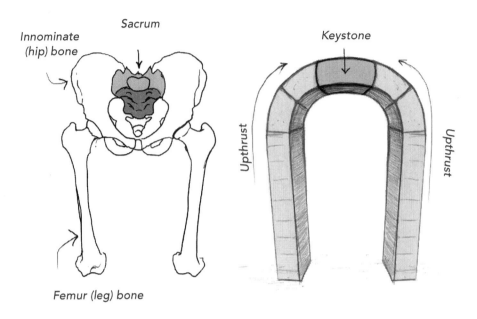

The pelvic arch with the sacrum as its keystone transmits the weight of the torso and head to the legs and carries upthrust through the leg bones to the primary axis.

The hip bone, the *pelvic girdle,* is officially a bone of the lower limbs, but because it is so solidly glued to the spine at the sacrum, it functions as part of the back. The pelvic girdle is comprised of the bilateral *innominate* bones, each a fusion of three bones that anchor the legs into the primary axis. The *pelvis* (meaning *basin*) is the pelvic girdle *plus* the bottom two sections of the spine, the sacrum and coccyx; together they form a fixed, stable ring that acts and moves as a single bone.

At the bottom of the pelvis, the rocker-like *sit bones* support the primary axis in sitting. The sit bones are 3-4" apart—you should be able to walk them forward and back on the seat of a chair. Like the feet, the sitbones extend into the earth in the direction opposite the head to conduct upthrust through the primary axis.

The feet are our contact with the earth; they support the primary axis off the ground and move it in space. The ***vertical axis*** extends from the soles of the feet to the crown of the head.

Each foot provides a tripod of support: the heel plus the knuckles* of the big and little toes. The foot's dome-like arches result when these three weight-bearing points conduct upthrust. The heels receive 50% of the weight; the big toes, most of the rest, while the outer bones balance and stabilize.

The foot has height—imagine it as a pyramid and note that the heel is well behind the ankle joint. The feet spread when bearing weight, allowing nerve receptors in their muscles and connective tissue to relay messages to the brain about balance.

The toes act as *buttresses,* ready to assist in balance when you are standing—the pads touch the ground but don't necessarily bear weight. The five toes together with their knuckles make a tunnel-like transverse arch for standing on the balls of your feet. In walking you roll through the ball; in running you push off it; in tango you pivot on it.

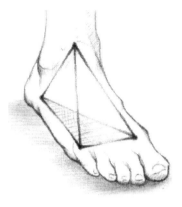

THE FOOT PYRAMID: Note the tripod of contact and support. Note also its height and that the heel is well behind the ankle joint.

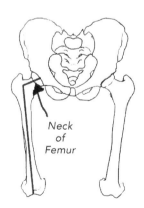

Neck of Femur

Articulation of the neck of the femur with the back/pelvis.

The **femur**, the big bone of the upper leg, articulates with the pelvis' hip socket via its neck, which angles inward almost 90° from the long bone. In walking, the bottom of the femur swings the knee forward from the primary axis.

The **knees and ankles** are both hinge joints that articulate over the first two toes. In restful standing the knees are neither locked nor bent and should have some play of movement.

---

* The knuckles of the foot are the heads of the metatarsals, right before the toes start.

Avant-garde dancer Merce Cunningham at fifty-one moving expansively in a 1970 performance.

The two lower leg bones move headward up off the top of the foot pyramid. Most of the ankles' play in movement (as in walking cobblestones or creeks) actually comes from the arch bones of the foot.

The aforementioned bones are the most important for understanding the main beam, the vertical axis, and upthrust. Other bones that participate in tensegrous volume include the ribs, upper limbs,* and the jaw.

The ribs hang off the back sides of the thoracic vertebrae to make a fabulously flexible cage that insures volume and protects the lung, heart, and innards. With the diaphragm, the ribs are a breathing machine whose rise and fall changes volume to create a vacuum that propels respiration. Getting the ribs to work led Alexander to his discoveries about the importance of length and volume to the *use* of the entire self.

The arms hang from the **shoulder girdle,** which perches at the top of the breast bone, a centerpiece of the hanging rib cage. The collar bones (clavicles) make a yoke for suspending the arms as far to the sides as possible. (More volume!) "Widening into the upper arms" is an Alexander *direction*. Alexander teacher Barbara Conable contends that "God designed the shoulder girdle so that man might play the violin."[9] Author Christopher McDougall says "Humans are amazing throwers. We are unique among all animals in our ability to throw projectiles at high speeds and with incredible accuracy. It's not in the muscles; women free of cultural bias can throw as well as men. The better we threw, the more intelligent we became."[10]

Elbows are heavy—they hang. **Forearms** are exactly long enough for the hands to reach the mouth without distorting the primary axis. **Wrists** are about two inches of ball-bearing shaped bones that give the hands a vast range of movement. The **hands** merit their own book—this book is concerned primarily with their weight-bearing role as forepaws.

The **jaw** hangs from the skull—it is a suspended limb of the skull, sliding forward as it hinges. The jaw joint is in intimate proximity to other key players in primary control: the balance organs of the inner ear and the AO joint. *Misuse* at the AO joint will often result in temporo-mandibular problems like "TMJ."

---

* The *limb girdles* grow in the womb in response to signals from the budding limbs, which they will anchor into the primary axis. The earliest movements of the limbs are totally integrated with trunk action. Don't distort the primary axis for the sake of action in the limbs.

THE ELASTIC STRINGS

Fascia connects everything and keeps the body from falling apart. Other connective tissues include muscle, tendons, ligaments, and cartilage. Muscle is actively sensitive to stretch and resists stretch that doesn't correspond to intention. Like fascia, muscle length changes with *use* over time, but muscle can also lengthen in an instant until constrained by the fascia surrounding it. When you stretch your muscles, you are actually stretching your fascia.

Tangueros—Note her torsion and both of their vertical axes.

Muscles are either flexors (in front) or extensors (in back). They are either red or white. The outer white muscles that move the bones are "quick-twitch" and fatigable—don't rely on them posturally, as they'll get tired and you'll slump.

The deep red postural muscles don't tire out. If not constantly used, however, they lose their red muscle quality and become fatigable. The less they are used, the less they can be used. Furthermore, if not used, their size decreases and "they lose the ability to take in sugar, interfering with optimum metabolism to create a downward spiral of well-being."[11] Red muscle likes rhythmic movement[12]—rocking and laughing feel good.

The Alexander Technique activates the deep postural muscles to do their job of stabilizing the bones so that the bones *can* conduct upthrust. The muscles and connective tissues spiral around the bones. Twisting and rotation result from the interaction between the flexors and extensors as well as the spherical structure of the muscles. Spirals accompany every movement. The contralateral spiral of the torso assures a headward orientation in smooth walking and running.

Rory McIlroy shows his fine golfing spiral while keeping the integrity of his primary axis.

These drawings show the spirals in the musculature, the outer (white) muscles wrapping the torso and the deep red *spiral line* tying the core together. The spiral line begins at the back of the head and wraps around the body in a double spiral, helping to maintain balance across all planes.

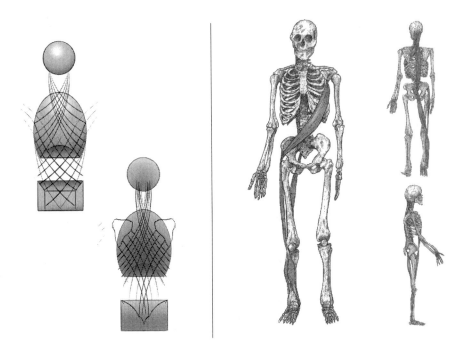

The spirals of the outer muscles of the torso on the left and the deep spiral line on the right.

If muscles shorten inappropriately, the nerves' main signaling system that organizes the tensegrity structure won't work and the bones will be prevented from contributing their weight to the system that wants volume. Consider that relaxing the muscles might allow you to experience the weight of the bones. If muscles shorten chronically, nerve receptors will no longer relay accurate information and kinesthesia will become "debauched." Alexander lessons "re-educate" the kinesthetic sense.

THE NERVES' FEEDBACK SYSTEM

Nerve Receptors and Reflexes

Nerve receptors are embedded throughout the muscles and connective tissue. They maintain a constant low-level tone in the muscles and generate continuous signals about position, motion, balance, and sway to the balance organs of the inner ear and the nerve receptors in the muscles and ligaments at the back of the neck.

Stretch reflexes start with contact with the ground. The feet must be allowed to spread in order to activate the muscles that hold us up by elastically supporting the skeleton. "If the stretch reflex network is not operating elastically, the muscular support system is not properly activated, and effortless support is replaced with chronic contraction of muscles, which are now needed to maintain upright posture."[13] Nerve sensors need the stretch to register changes and respond appropriately.

"Stretch reflexes maintain muscle tone. When you are awake and alert, they trigger contraction and a series of reflex actions to the spinal column that activate involuntary *postural reflexes.* This involuntary feedback loop of the stretch reflex *can* be mediated by intention."[14]

One of our oldest and strongest reflexes is the *righting reflex,* the innate desire for the head to be level. You can see it in a cat falling. (Interrupting this reflex, by pulling his head back and down, is how the cowboy throws the steer.)

Connective tissue is full of nerve sensors that depend on muscle elasticity for reliable feedback. A healthy reflex system in turn tones the whole body. In a properly balanced tensegrity structure, we can trust our senses.

TO SUMMARIZE

Our bodies seek ongoing postural equilibrium. However, we can go wrong in all three main components of the body's tensile balance: in the bones, by not using points of contact with the ground; in the muscles, by extra tension or lack of tone; and in a reflex system that has become unreliable.

Use affects function, therefore health and well-being. If we stop being "uptight," we can relax into an elastic system of antagonistic pulls, giving us a

Alexander helping toddler to suspend his body from his head.

sense of lightness, fullness and even buoyancy.

"Instead of thinking of gravity's downward pull, allow the planet to support you. The more we use gravity, the more we get what we need."[15] "Instead of trying to hold ourselves up, we can get up by releasing our holdings-down. When we un-grip to let ourselves go up and open out, we allow an expansion to come in."[16]

To quote anatomist and Alexander scholar, David Gorman, "The body is a suspension system. Everything is hung from everything else. The muscles suspend the skeleton, which rests on the ground which supports it and from which it extends upwards as a long spacer to spread apart the muscles which in turn respond to the stretches by suspending the body lightly down to the ground upon which it is supported..."[17]

The skeletal muscles become spring-loaded when you are lengthening your main beam. The fascia then has an elastic recoil energy. If not interfered with, the muscle tone of the whole body can be automatically organized at a reflex level. "Our inherent instability is not a design fault and thus a postural problem to be solved, but rather an essential part of our freedom and responsiveness."[18]

"Equilibrium is a dynamic and ongoing process."[19] When connective tissue and bones are balanced, the structure is stable with a lot of give—it has *resiliency*.

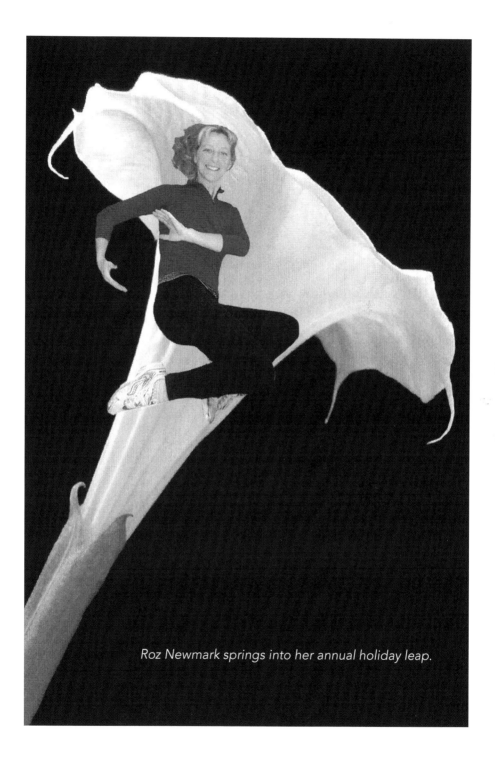

Roz Newmark springs into her annual holiday leap.

Look at how the leaping cat's lengthening impetus begins high up and way, way back.

The work is about freedom to change.

– Elisabeth Walker

Don't worry about it —it's only change.

– Marj Barstow

Once we change, slowly we get used to it.

– Jeremy Chance

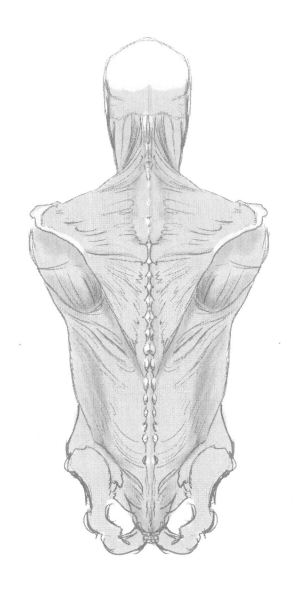

Get the back to work
and the legs will take care of themselves.

– FM Alexander

CHAPTER 8

Lifetime Habits
for Well-being

The adult learns to cultivate the skills of an infant, while the infant sees that it's OK to be on the floor—that there is no hurry to walk.

This chapter presents practices and strategies for *good use:* a few floor and upright exercises, hints for not injuring yourself, the primary axis redux, attitudes in Alexander lessons, and some moving meditations. Spend time on the floor, soak up the information in this book, and take a few Alexander lessons.

PRACTICES for *good use*

Spend time on the floor cultivating the skills of an infant. Many doctor-prescribed exercises for bad backs are effective because they are versions of what infants do. Most of you will prefer to lie on a softer surface like a rug or carpet; standard yoga mats will be too small for rolling.

Start on your back. Give weight to the floor so you can cease holding and tightening. *You can't fall off the floor.* Allow yourself to do nothing. Observe and trust the supporting surface of the floor to aid in the release of muscular tension; use the plane of the floor to find the plane of your back. (Do you understand the Alexander *direction* "back back"?)

Let your time on the floor be in the spirit of *pandiculation,* the act of stretching and yawning. Yawn and stretch all the way to your fingers and toes. Use the floor to massage your back.

Flexibility is not about touching toes or doing splits and backbends—it is the ability to fold the major joints of the body. Find the folds; explore articulations, investigating range of movement one limb at a time, while keeping your sacrum and lumbar spine still (or not).

Cultivate the idea of *greasing up the vertebral spools.* Let mindfulness soften the floor—rolling softly requires awareness of where you are NOW, at each moment in time and space. When lying down, identify your contact with the floor and let your body relax into it. In all upright activities, sitting in a chair, standing, and walking, ask: "What is my contact with the ground? Do I trust it? Am I moving up off of it?" And always: "Is my neck free? Can I do less?"

While lying on your back, learn to roll your head without tightening the neck muscles or distorting your torso. Then allow your eyes to lead your head and body into rotation and rolling. Eventually initiate from the other end as well, letting your hips and legs lead. Once you realize you can safely twist and spiral with the support of the floor, slowly begin to find the rolls.

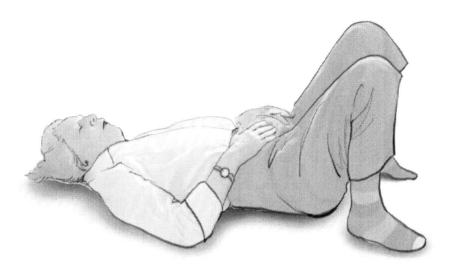

Cultivate the semi-supine habit

Make a habit of lying down in semi-supine for 10-15 minutes several times a week to rejuvenate the discs of your spine as you lengthen and widen your back. Venture small movements monitoring whether you can do them without tightening or shortening. Move one knee (the apex of a triangle from the foot and back) side to side without gripping the groin muscles or abandoning the contact of the sole of the foot with the floor. Try straightening one leg at a time while keeping your heel in contact with the floor. Try bringing one leg up to your chest. Try humming or vocalizing vowel sounds without tightening the back of your neck.

To soothe your back without paying so much attention, prop your knees up with a big pillow or rest your calves on a chair seat so the femur is at about a right angle to the floor.*

---

* Remember you may need to put books under your head when lying on your back; if the back of your head can't reach the floor without pulling your head back and down, put something under it.

The *sit bone stretch*

On your back, in the supine fetal fold (knees and hips folded), with arms

on the floor angling out above your head or to the sides, "walk" the sit bones away from your head. Let the reach of your sit bones in one direction and your hands/arms in the opposite bring your whole body into a stretch. Revel in that longitudinal stretch. Begin with your legs folded, but notice how they can eventually participate so that their extended weight magnifies the movement and the stretch.

Supine fetal fold.

The sit bone stretch is a delicious way to massage and stretch your back.

If you can't keep your legs folded while lying on your back, walk your sit bones as close as possible to a wall and put the soles of your feet against the wall to maintain the folds of your legs. Enliven the soles of your feet, finding a little bit of push, while you explore wall-assisted variations of the *sit bone stretch*.

Lying on the floor should be a delicious experience!

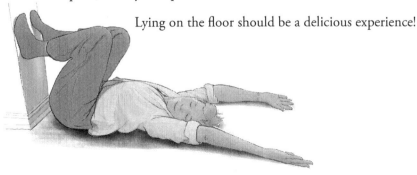

Explore prone positions. Become aware of the weight-bearing potential of your forearms and palms. Venture an infant pushup without tightening your back, bottom, or feet. Turn this into pre-crawling by activating the toes and encouraging them to seek purchase. How might this compare with reptilian movement?

With the eyes leading, look around to engage your peripheral vision. When the eyes look up and around, your body may be lured to roll over onto your back. (This surprises infants when it first happens to them.)

Pentapodal = five points of contact and support. The head must maintain contact with the floor, but let it roll to experience different angles of upthrust into the rounded spine. Find the little rocks from side to side and from head to tail.

Child's Pose = kowtow = pentapodal = five points of contact. Find upthrust through the contact of the head, which can roll; let it roll, while maintaining contact with the ground. Explore and enjoy the C-shaped stretch of the spine's curve, making it tighter or looser. Feel the changes in contact, upthrust, and the curvature of the spine as you make changes like raising your bottom. Find the tiny oscillations and rocks, both head to tail and side to side.

Crawl Position

When you begin to crawl, add in cat-like undulations in all planes.

From the pillars of "all fours," find the "crawl cone." Play with its circularity and how that invites the legs to fold, giving the cone a different orientation.

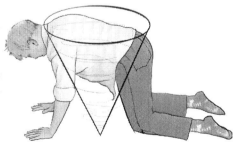

107

General Attitude in upright

• Notice habits that diminish your stature.

• Trust your feet.

• Point or aim up with the brainstem.

• Feel the opposition between the soles of your feet and the top of your head. If I push down on the crown of your head, could you feel that in your feet? Could you meet my force without tightening? Could you feel the spring of your spine? Can you feel gravity in the soles of your feet? And upthrust through the points of contact with the ground?

• Find your axis. Are your knees soft? Can you move them back and forth without actually bending them?

• Think your AO joint so far back (and up) that the sub-occipital muscles can be tensile—not contracted, but delicately stretched.

• Maintain spaciousness in the AO joint in each and every moment.

• Don't try to straighten the spinal curves.

• Look outward. Invite visual awareness to the retinae at the back of the eyes.*

• Find the cone of movement of your vertical axis as detailed on page 59. Note the core strength recruited to keep the axis intact. Notice where the arcs of your cone are jagged.

• Keep the sit bones in line with the ears. Let your sit bones dangle when standing.

• Imagine "sitting on a bucket" to keep the feet active and engaged. The verticality of the primary axis moving up off the sit bones has a sense of uprightness and delicacy.

---

* Peter Grunwald recommends you bring this visual receptiveness all the way through the optic nerve to the optical cortex at the back of the brain—a good idea.

• Adopt an erect "listening posture" to let sounds and images come into you.

• Don't lead with the face.

• Observe. Ask whether crawling is an option.

• Practice *monkey*. Allow a hint of *monkey* in upright activities. Sit to stand, stand to sit.

• Think expansion and space. Prohibit narrowing and shortening.

• Notice what is unnecessary. Let go of excess tension and banish distortion.

• Ask, what is my contact with the ground? Do I trust it? Am I moving up off it? (Up and away, headward, away from the sit bones and the ankles.)

• Remember tensegrity. View weight as the opposite of tension. By NOT HOLDING, by letting the bones be heavy, the muscles allow the tensegrity structure its optimum space, spring, and mechanical advantage.

• Using a cane or walker: Don't lean on it, but push off instead. Let the connection through your "forepaws" to the ground help you to find your back and your feet. Look outward—focus on your target, not on the ground.

The Senses Game

This was a game that Indian or pioneer girls played in the prairie grasses—something I read in a novel. They would stand in the tall grass with eyes, ears, and nose as high as possible and call out, as fast as possible, all the things they could see, hear, and smell.

Presence up!

– Christopher Neville

STRATEGIES for *good use*

FM Alexander 'checking his messages'

• Using a hand-held digital device: Let voice recognition software do your texting for you. Avoid "texting-neck" by being mindful of the inherent *misuse* of digital screen time. Don't diminish your stature or compromise your primary axis to do something that can be accomplished in other ways.

Our forearms just aren't long enough to bring a device to eye level without raising the elbows—elbows are heavy and prefer not to be raised for long periods of time. Bring your eyes in line with your device by tilting your head forward at the AO joint instead of bending the whole neck forward from the back. Try the creative-use-of-pillows strategy suggested for reading books and magazines.

Creative use of pillows

• Reading while sitting: Creative use of pillows—build a mountain of pillows on your lap to bring reading material to eye level.

• Sleeping: Be as flexible as infants. Sleeping on your back, sides, and front are all viable options, but switch it up. Use pillows under the knees when you're on your back and under the head when on your side. Get out of bed with a roll to the side to push 4-leggedly up onto your forearms and palms.

• Driving a car: Adjust car seats so you are upright, not reclining. You may have to reverse the headrest to keep the primary axis on one plane. Because the backs of so many car seats are concave, you may want to keep a jacket or pillow handy to stuff behind your back.

• Watching a movie: The new theater seats are worse than ever—use same strategies as when dealing with car seats.

• Using computers: Keep your eyes level—the screen should be at or slightly below eye-level. Wear eyeglasses that give perfect vision at about a 25-inch range. Don't push your face forward.

• Wearing glasses: Make sure the glasses fit. Don't tilt the head backward to keep them from falling onto your nose. Verify that bifocal lines are in the right place so you don't have to pull your head back and down to see out of the close-up zone.

• Playing musical instruments: Don't "practice" your instrument, but instead work on yourself through the activity of playing the instrument. Resist end-gaining. The Suzuki violin teaching method doesn't let kids play their instruments for the first year–they learn only to pick them up without tension or distortion.

• Riding a bicycle. You can rotate your head up from the atlanto-occipital joint without pulling it back and down.

• Correcting bad posture: If you notice you are slumping, AT teacher and scholar Ron Dennis recommends you "do a teeny wilt, then lengthen out of it."[1]

Even the fastest animal doesn't hurry.

– Carol Gill

Olympic marathoner Ryan Hall

Take Alexander lessons

Alexander lessons are a rewiring process where you learn not-to-do postural habits of a lifetime. Lessons call attention to habits of *misuse*. Take a few lessons, if only for curiosity's sake. *www.alexandertechniqueworldwide.com* links you to teachers anywhere in the world.

Discover why the Alexander experience helps you understand the process. Give change time. Try different teachers. Consider lessons to be an investigation into your maximum well-being.

Start noticing. Awareness is the first key. Which postural habits undermine your support? "Letting go" is so important; be willing to *not do* your habit in order to experience something new.

Alexander considered our ability to control our *use* to be *man's supreme inheritance*. "It is the choices we make about the way we conduct ourselves every day that determine the quality of our lives."[2]

> Let's face it: if you *misuse* yourself, ten years
> down the line you're just not going to feel as well
> as someone who *uses* himself well.
>
> – Giora Pinkas

Movement Meditations

Any activity, from walking and swimming to chopping onions and washing dishes, can be a movement meditation. Moving meditations are easier than just sitting, as there is more to keep track of, more to keep the brain from wandering. Nevertheless, when your mind does wander, bring it back to the ongoing present without judgment. In every moment give attention to how you use yourself and weed out excess tension. Trust the feet and your contact with the ground.

Martial arts have "kata," short choreographed repeatable pieces that are essentially moving meditations. Most highlight the *integrity of the primary axis* as well as the vertical axis from the soles of the feet to the top of the head. They include the yin and yang principles of opposition.

The predominant standing posture in the martial arts is a variation of the lunge with one foot in front of the other. Taiji's lunge places the feet far apart so that the knees bend deeply and the primary axis moves long distances with each change of weight. Aikido's lunge stance may be more subtle in order to cultivate a body language that will disarm a fight before it begins. In most martial arts the arms embrace an imaginary "sphere of power" in the front of the torso, as if carrying a big box.

Taiji, more commonly known as *tai chi*, is a wonderful movement meditation. It is especially helpful for older beginners who are new to exercise. It builds the core, the deep red postural muscles, while increasing aerobic capacity. You can do it anywhere and don't need a partner. It is so slow that you can practice its principles discretely in a grocery store line. It should be done in the spirit of a cat stalking prey.

Taiji is basically moving the vertical primary axis back and forth from one foot to the other in a slow, comfortable rhythm while staying as low as possible, as if sitting in a chair. Be relaxed. Put your mind at your center of gravity (2-3 inches below the navel and ⅔ of the way back). The primary axis, with shoulders over hips, moves as a single piece. It may rotate in relationship to the legs, but it doesn't twist. Arms ride on the movement created by the primary axis; the *sphere of power*, whose size can change, always stays in front.

In taiji's lunge position, the feet maintain shoulder width, with the distance between the feet no greater than can accommodate a smooth transfer of weight. The greater the length of the step, the further the primary axis can travel. One's center should stay at the same height, with no distortion or tension, while the primary axis is transferred slowly and mindfully from front foot to back foot. Taiji positions can be held—it doesn't take long to feel the burn in your quads. Note that the stillness has movement within it.

Taiji players in lunge, sparring: "pushing, sensing, or circling hands." Both players maintain the verticality and integrity of their primary axes.

Taiji's *bear* is an excellent meditation. It is a warmup exercise with minimum choreography. Stand with feet parallel and shoulder-width apart, knees bent, back vertical. The soles of the feet will always maintain their contact with the ground.

Start with weight 50/50 then slowly let it all pour into one foot while the empty foot maintains contact with the ground. With the weight all on one foot, rotate the primary axis slowly around itself—toward the standing leg and back a few times. Let the hanging arms ride on that circular movement, gently swinging around the turning primary axis.

Then, without changing height, pour the weight into the other foot and repeat. The feet keep their root and the knees are still. The primary axis stays vertical and distortion-free. Find a slow, comforting rhythm, moving from side to side while rotating around your primary axis.

Most of **aikido** is done in a lunge position (*hanmi*) with one foot in front of the other. Like taiji, aikido's "rowing exercise" shifts the weight from front to back foot, but with less emphasis on keeping the primary axis absolutely vertical. With power centered in the lower abdomen, imagine pushing and pulling a car, while allowing the arms to ride on the back-and-forth movement of the center.

Tango's home base brings the heels together, so that the vertical axis will barely move when the weight is transferred 100% from foot to foot. With the weight all on one foot, the empty foot should be able to explore its full peripheral range while maintaining contact with the floor. The standing leg holds the axis steady in the center; knee bend can vary, affecting the distance the free foot can move away from the axis. As with ballet's *barre work*, moving the leg away from a stable center strengthens the core.

In tango's *disassociation* the primary axis twists around itself, while in taiji the primary axis rotates as a single piece. The tango embrace keeps the arms right in front of the torso just like the martial art *sphere of power*.

Yoga is also a movement meditation that fosters strength and flexibility, although it doesn't necessarily clearly highlight the integrity of the primary axis the way these other movement practices do.

For the simplest of movement meditations, **follow your breath.** Do it anytime, anywhere, in little snippets of time. Focus on any of the many possible aspects of the breathing process—a good starting place is to notice the passage of air at the rim of the nostrils. Recent studies show that a simple breathing meditation helps children learn.

Alexander's *directions* are also useful meditations anywhere, any time. They promote *good use* by encouraging the body to lengthen, widen, and expand. They bring awareness to the head/neck/back relationship, the primacy of the back, and the importance of releasing tension. Free your neck so your head can move up and away, making room for your body to follow. Entertaining the notion of crawling will insure that you are *directing*.

Final thoughts about movement

Alexander's *directions* are also directions in three-dimensional space. They encourage your body to take up as much space as possible: lengthening, widening, and expanding multi-directionally. Think volume. Think every major joint to move away from every other major joint.

Consider the parallels between Alexander's *direction* and Eastern medicine/philosophy's principle of extending ki/qi.

Visualize dogs and horses rolling around on their backs. Oh, how good it feels to lie down!

Get on the floor. Nurture our old and intimate relationship with the ground and gravity.

Observe connections between emotions and muscular tension. Does the emotion create the posture or does the posture create the emotion?

Remind yourself of all the fantastic things a flexible spine can do. Not only does it spiral, but it undulates.

More tensegrity images: A balloon, with its squishable rigidity. A flexible mold of jello that doesn't lose its shape. A suspension bridge. A clothes line.

Realize we live a constant dance of juggling the opposition between stability and mobility.

Stop. Take a break. Relax. Practice doing nothing beyond observing breath, weight, contact with the earth, and sensory input.

It is hard to be tense or anxious if
your muscles are not tense.

– David Garlick

Quotes

These are organized loosely by author categories: Alexander; his first teachers alphabetically by last name; contemporary AT teachers alphabetically; and finally scientists and non-Alexander teachers. Unattributed quotes are either common knowledge or from my student notebooks. *Few of these quotes appear in the text of the book.* At the end of this appendix are a few short definitions/explanations of the Alexander Technique.

FM ALEXANDER

- The most valuable knowledge we can possess is of the use and functioning of the self.

- Change involves carrying out an activity against the habit of life.

- As we grow up and our habits of movement develop, they become the masters of our movement.[1]

- Inhibition is the cornerstone of the technique.

- *It's all about breathing, but don't mention the word.*

- You don't want to be right, but to learn to meet a stimulus that always puts you wrong and to deal with it.

- Habit need not be mindless. It should be plastic and creative.

- You are getting away from all your old preconceived ideas because you are getting away from your old habits.

- Belief is a certain standard of muscular tension.[2]

- Talk about a man's individuality and character—it's the way he uses himself.

- You can't do something you don't know if you keep on doing what you do know.

- As soon as you don't care whether you're right or wrong, the impeding obstacle is gone.

- End-gaining always throws you into the habitual.

- The true objective of lessons is to launch a person upon a course of self-discovery, which leads to increased awareness and control.

- Conscious control of *use* is man's supreme inheritance.

- Get the back to work and the legs will take care of themselves.

- The growing child should have a balanced state in which inhibition and volition develop equally. Kids must not fear failure; learning must not be charged with emotional fears. The student should tend primarily to the means whereby.

- Happiness is defined as doing well at something that interests you.

- If you hold yourself to the position that was RIGHT yesterday, where does the possibility of change come in?

- I am not interested in the particular manifestation of your wrongness. We are working on a principle whereby we tend to get rid of not one of our peculiarities but the lot.[3]

- If we become sensorily aware of doing a harmful thing to ourselves, we can cease doing it.[4]

- I never stop working on myself—I dare not.[5]

FM Alexander

119

FIRST GENERATION ALEXANDER TEACHERS

AR Alexander

- Of course *directions* are doings, but they are small, usually below the sense register.[6]

Marj Barstow

- If you're directing, you *are* inhibiting.

- Forget about right and wrong—concern yourself with what is unnecessary.

- Constructive thinking allows you to move your head in a slightly upward direction in such a manner that your whole body has room to follow, room to move and get rid of your slump.

- You are using your constructive thinking to get rid of the downward pressures.

- Let the whole mechanism move up, starting at the head.

- The only way to free the neck is by moving the head.

- It takes constructive thinking to redirect your energy—if you can catch yourself, you can change.

- The legs and the feet just tag along.

- Don't worry about it—it's only change.

- Your thinking is far more delicate than my hands could ever be.

- Just a little bit of ease.

- It's not a position, it's a movement.

- There is nothing wrong with your slump; it is part of your flexibility. The problem is that you do it all the time—you have no choice.

The two Marj's (Marjory Barlow and Marj Barstow) at the 2nd International Congress in 1988.

- If you want to keep squashing yourself, go ahead. Nobody cares.

- Lengthening is the result of the loss of your slump.

- Your feet should touch the floor as delicately as your head moves forward and up.

- A stiffened neck will affect every major movement. "When there is an interference with the ease and flexibility of the poise of the head at the top of the spine, there is interference with the natural quality of movement of the entire mechanism."[7]

- Don't decide that something is hard or difficult or it will be.

Marjory Barlow

- You cannot change and still remain the same. You're not going to be able to go down path B unless you stop going down path A.

- FM used to say, "When you're changing, you get discomfort that is close to pain."

- The suboccipital muscles are the "handmaids of the cranial globe."[8]

- You have to not be afraid of being wrong and have to give up wanting to be right.

- If you react straight away, you will do what you've always done.[9]

- One thing you can do, notice how you never say no. How you rush from one thing to another and you never have a pause. Just notice that.[10]

- It is as if each of us is trying to take up the least possible amount of room in the universe.

Marjory (née Mecham) Barlow and Wilfred Barlow celebrating the publication of Will's 1973 book, The Alexander Principle.

121

Dilys Carrington[11]

- All of the joints release at the same time, just after the neck has been released by dropping the nose, *which you do upwards.*

- *Directing* means getting internal length and stretch throughout the body. *Inhibition* is not doing those things that interfere with lengthening. *Direction* is a continuous process of self-monitoring.

Walter Carrington

- I really think I prefer 'going up' to 'pulling down.'[12]

Dilys Carrington (ca. 1984)

Eric de Peyer[13]

- The mere thought of an activity is sufficient to ennervate the muscles which habitually perform that activity.

- There must be mental neutrality about doing the act or there will always be a preliminary mobilization along the lines of the existing habit/pattern.

- A predisposition to certain psychological states is perpetuated by the physical habits which belong to them. You must receive from an outside source the experience of a different pattern.

- If we habitually adopt a depressed posture, we are already depression-prone.

Walter Carrington waxing

Margaret Goldie

- What you think is what you get.[14]

Patrick Macdonald

- Aim up and stay back under all conditions.[15]

- Up to go up, up to go down. Up to go into *monkey*.

- Faulty *use* is present in most cases of illness and disease.

- *Direction* has the two meanings of "to order" and "to point," Alexander's use of the word includes both meanings.[16]

- The Alexander Technique is interested in the orientation of the body as a prerequisite to the movement in space.[17]

- (Quoting a boxing teacher of his youth) I can teach you to do this, but I can't learn you. You will have to learn yourself."[18]

Patrick Macdonald

Peter Scott

- In Alexander's work there are no right positions, only right conditions.

Sir George Trevelyan

- Each lesson gave one the extraordinary taste of what *right use* might mean. One walked as on air after a lesson.

Elisabeth Walker

- The work is about freedom to change.

Lulie Westfeldt

- When a person has held beliefs for a number of years, they have become habits of thought.

Kitty Wielopolska

- Let the eyes be free to go apart. See from the point of vision.

- Alexander understood Reich's theory that physically breaking up the armoring of the musculature would create the possibility for change in character. He believed that his Work, if pursued long enough, acted as [psycho]analysis, an enormous claim to make.[19]

First generation teachers, Dick and Elisabeth Walker in the late 1930's atop Crib Goch in North Wales.

- Don't control the breathing. Let the body do the breathing.

- The Alexander orders seem to be a way of getting back to the original hardwiring.

- Thinking influences what happens in your muscles.

CONTEMPORARY ALEXANDER TEACHERS

Ed Avak

- Consider the jackhammerer and a child and the difference in the quality of their respective touch.

Larry Ball

- Movement is implicit in the spiral.

- Do less. Take that concept inside your body and it becomes a vibrant activity.

Goddard Binkley

- My early family experience of rejection and my own physical tendency to collapse produced a pattern of submissiveness, lack of confidence, and self doubt.

- More and more I see that the difficulties and problems of life are mostly obstacles of our own making. To see this is the beginning of freedom.

Bob Britton

- Let's look at the bigger picture.

- I tense, therefore I am. (facetiously)

Bob Britton shows the way.

Jeremy Chance, guest teacher at the Alexander Training Institute in San Francisco in the late 1980s.

- When the pain of continuing the way I am is greater than the pain of changing, I'll change. Once we change, slowly we get used to it.

- We all want to change, but most of us would like to be able to stay the same while we do so. We must give up what we know and step into the unfamiliar.

Remy Charlip

- The head leading the torso into space is the "means whereby" in any movement.

- The sit bones are the feet of the torso.

Rivka Cohen:

- Be up there. (I call it the penthouse.)

- Aim up and stay back under all conditions, both in poise and in movement.

- The ground activates the reflexes to go up. Ground brings the power of opposition. I call this "direction in action." With it we can move into space with the dynamic of the power of opposition.[20]

Barbara Conable:

- The proximity, the relationship, of the top of the spine with the top of the jaw is the *Beacon Hill of the body*.

Aileen Crow:

- Emotional factors enter into the process of change. To alter one's equilibrium is to change one's state of consciousness, body attitude, and self image.

Pedro de Alcantara

- Are you ready for anything and everything? Are you well-directed, like a cat doing nothing and yet ready to spring into action at a microsecond's notice?[21]

- As I see it, to direct is to sense energy, to gather it within, to dispense it outwardly, to project it, to use it, to receive it, to share it.[22]

John Coffin

- The F. Matthias Alexander Technique is a means for teaching the child or adult an improved use of himself as a whole. The pupil is shown what he is unconsciously doing that interferes with his best performance of any activity. As he comes to recognize his wrong, habitual reaction, he learns how consciously to prevent it, and thus provides himself with a control that makes for the greatest efficiency possible at any stage of his development. It is a control that he will be able to use in whatever he is doing or learning, whether arithmetic or tennis, since his chief instrument in any activity is the same, namely himself.[23]

Ted Dimon

- In order for the postural system to work properly, we must be awake, alert, and actively involved.

Jack Fenton

- The popular conception of posture gives no hint of how vital a person's posture is to his effectiveness, well-being, and enjoyment.

- If the eyes alone will do, then use the eyes.

- Make haste slowly. New habits require time and constant repetition.

Bruce Fertman from Marj Barstow workshop summer 1977

- That forward undertow movement that collects the whole body upward. [In reference to the ideal forward and up movement of the head.]

- *Up* is multi-directional, like bread rising.

Jean M.O. Fischer

- The change of habits brings about the unexpected, the truly new as opposed to the anticipated new. A journal records not only physical changes, but also changes in concept, attitude and outlook on oneself and life in general; these are, perhaps, more slowly attained and problematic to articulate.

David Garlick in talk at 2nd International Congress in Brighton, England in 1987.

- There is an important interplay between the state of muscle and the state of mind. Muscle gets patterns that can perpetuate "mood states." It is hard to be tense or anxious if your muscles are not tense.

- The more that muscles are contracted, the less we are able to detect what the muscles and associated tissues and joints are doing. Contracted muscles decrease proprioceptive activity.

- Even snakes yawn. (The yawn = an expression of equilibrium between tension and relaxation.)[24]

Michael Gelb

- Alexander realized that the choices we make about what we do with ourselves to a large extent determine the quality of our lives.

Carol Gill

- Even the fastest animal doesn't hurry.

- Let the sit bones dangle slightly behind the knees.

David Gorman

- Instead of thinking of gravity's downward pull, allow the planet to support you. The more we use it, the more we get what we need.[25]

- The joints of the spine are distortion joints. The discs are flexible and elastic. There is no movement in your spine without the discs being distorted in some way—squashed, bent, twisted, or stretched.[26]

Kay Hogan

- Anything you can teach to the right hand, you can teach to the left.

Frank Pierce Jones

- Refusal to give consent to habitual response is the basic means for change.

- Alexander realized that his doing was his undoing.

- In the narrower sense, *use* describes posture as it changes over time. In the broader sense, *use* describes the total pattern of behavior in the ongoing present.

Shoshana Kaminitz

- Holding your breath sabotages everything.

Judith Liebowitz

- *Inhibition* is implicit in *direction*, and if you are *directing* properly, you must have already successfully inhibited your habitual response.[27]

- The head is poised, not positioned.[28]

- The Alexander Technique is experiential; It needs to be experienced to be understood.

- If you've never been there, you don't know what to expect.

- Freedom is being able to make a choice of behavior unburdened by the chains of habit.

Ann Mathews

- Life is in one sense body mechanics.[29]

Kelly McEvenue

- The butt is the back.

Louise Morgan

- The power of conscious control over his movements and actions by changing habits is man's supreme inheritance.

Alex Murray

- I've seen people get along without feet, but not without a head.

John Nicholls

- You have to be willing to fall apart.

- If someone has gone around for 35 years with certain patterns of muscular tension, then that's bound to feel normal.[30]

Frank Ottiwell with Marj Barstow and the author at the 2nd International Congress in Brighton, England in 1988.

Frank Ottiwell

- Articulation is more fun.

- There are 26 bones in the foot [or 206 bones in the body] and they're all moving away from each other.

- We are not hanging—we are being thrust up.

- Use the head in such a way that you get the greatest possible lengthening of the spine in each and every action.

- *Widening* is an absence of narrowing. Be willing to do anything but narrow.

- *Widening* image of brushing the skyscrapers with shoulders while walking through the canyons of New York City.

- I like to think of it (the primary control) as the *primary activity*.

- You are your only instrument—you don't even have a violin to carry.

- When I can bring myself to allow *being* to be primary (instead of doing), end-gaining ceases to be an issue.

> You are your only instrument—
> you don't even have a violin to carry.
>
> – Frank Ottiwell

Glen Park

- The starting point of the Alexander Technique is stopping, doing nothing.

Giora Pinkas

- Let's face it: if you *misuse* yourself, ten years down the line you're just not going to feel as well as someone who uses himself well.

Cathy Pollock

- Find the feet; follow the head.

Phyllis Richmond

- The crux of the matter is to inhibit the immediate response of "trying to get it right" so that we have a chance to make a reasoned change. Seriously engaging in the process of change requires commitment, practice, and an ability to tolerate the unknown. [31]

- We tend to think we know how to move better than our bodies do, so with all good intentions, we interfere with our *use*. Repetition of the interference strengthens the *misuse*. It is not possible to "do" good *use*—it happens by itself when we do not interfere with it.[32]

- You are learning to take advantage of a two-tenths of a second window to stop a habit that interferes with the coordinated activity of reflexes and other mechanisms that influence postural support and movement, so that you can be spontaneously and unpredictably creative![33]

Dr. Christopher H. H. Stevens

- The postural system has widespread links to many seemingly separate physical and psychological aspects of behavior.[34]

Joyce Woodman

- Actors are athletes.

SCIENTISTS, THINKERS, AUTHORS, MOVERS

Samuel Avital

- The vibration of singing gives life to every cell of the body.

Bonnie Bainbridge Cohen

- Babies are practicing all the time.

Professor Cheng man Ch'ing

- The physiological basis of character is posture, specifically the carriage of the head.

- The softer the body, the quicker the movement.

George Coghill

- As the animal grows, the limbs acquire partial independence, but are always dependent for their adequate performance on the maintenance of the total pattern of the trunk.[35]

Raymond Dart

- In human beings the head moves in order to extend the range of vision; to better his vision, man became completely upright. Perhaps the richest comedy presented by the evolutionary process is that the creature's nature, designed to have perfect posture and vision, should today present a picture of bespectacled decrepitude.[36]

- The musculature can be understood as double spirals wrapping around a flexible central axis.

- The basic discovery Alexander made from 1888 onwards was the practice of deliberate conscious inhibition.[37]

Robertson Davies

• The Alexander Technique keeps the body alive at ages when many people have resigned themselves to irreversible decline.

John Dewey, left, with FM Alexander c. 1920.

John Dewey

• As Mr. Alexander points out, one uses the very conditions that need re-education as a standard of judgment.[38]

• A person gets old because he bends over.

• We must stop thinking of standing up straight.

• *The Alexander Technique bears the same relationship to education that education itself bears to all other human activities.*

• Habitual *misuse* eventually finds its expression in a posture or in a limited repertoire of postures which come to dominate a person's character. In small and unobtrusive ways we become enslaved to our past.

Laura Huxley

- The Alexander Technique is not a method of accumulating information nor the art of learning something new. It is, instead, the art of UNLEARNING, which is much more subtle and, sometimes, a more difficult endeavor—unlearning that which is habitual instead of natural—letting go of old patterns and of those repetitive opinions arrived at in times and circumstances totally different from those of the present.

John Lilly

- The limits of your belief define the limits of your reality.

Peter Macdonald M.D praising Alexander in his 1924 inaugural address as chairman of the British Medical Association.

- Alexander is a teacher pure and simple. He does not profess to treat disease at all. ... [With lessons] manifestations of disease, however, *do* disappear.

J.E.R McDonaugh MD (one of the "nineteen doctors" who petitioned the British Medical Association to include AT training in the curriculum for training doctors) after meeting Alexander and watching his technique:

- It became apparent to me that the *wrong use* of the body plays an important role in disease.[39]

Ken McKenna

- Indecision is the key to flexibility.

Christopher Neville

- Presence up.

- The body's tensegrity is a spring-loaded symphony.

Marion Rosen

- What happens if you contract every muscle of your body? You stop breathing and you get smaller. So get big again; get as big as you can allow yourself to be.

Sir Charles Sherrington[40]

- Any path we trace in the brain leads directly or indirectly to muscle.

- To refrain from an act is no less an act than to commit one, because inhibition is co-equally with excitation a nervous activity.

Nikolaas Tinbergen in his 1973 Nobel acceptance speech:

- We [he, his wife, and a daughter] already notice, with growing amusement, very striking improvements in such diverse things as high blood pressure, depth of sleep, overall cheerfulness and mental alertness, resilience against outside pressures, and also in such a refined skill as playing a musical instrument.

- Alexander discovered that a lifelong *misuse* of the body muscles can make the entire system go wrong. As a consequence, messages that 'all is correct' received by the brain are not necessarily so.

- The innumerable muscles of the body are continuously operating as an intricately linked web.

Three prominent American Alexander teachers at Pamela Blanc's graduation in 1979. Course directors Giora Pinkas on our left and the late Frank Ottiwell on the right.

Mabel Todd

- Hold less, balance more.

- Wherever there's a joint, recall the possibilities for motion.

- The nearer the center the parts are supported, the further away from the center they can move in organized movement.

- Man must now regain his primitive awareness in a cellular sense. As less energy is expended in holding unbalanced positions, more is released for movement.

- The mechanisms for moving on land and breathing on land developed together.

- Although no one position may be entirely incorrect or correct, some are known to be better than others because they result in less strain and fatigue. This factor alone ultimately affects the well-being of the individual.

Alfred North Whitehead

- Your perception is entirely dependent on how your body is functioning.

Buddhist

- You must not care.

- If you feel that the teacher is a real teacher, then give up your own ideas and learn.[41]

Anonymous

- If it weren't for time, we'd have to do everything all at once.[42]

I can teach you to do this, but I can't learn you. You will have to learn yourself.

– Patrick Macdonald

A few short, easy-to-grasp explanations of the AT

- Alexander called it "psychophysical re-education."

- It's all about the back, the integrity of the back and our evolution as vertebrate animals. The back organizes the whole.

- Actors study it. It gives them poise, choice, and range.

- A musician's instrument sounds better when there is less tension in the player's body.

- Dancers (tangueros, martial artists) all work with axis and balance.

- The Alexander teacher is concerned with establishing positive conditions for health.

- A means to free ourselves from habitual interference with our own 'righting reflexes.'[43]

- The method for keeping your eye on the ball applied to life.[44]

Cartoons, Pictures, and Images

Alexander neither used nor believed in images. He was adamant that we be present in the here-and-now. Images, however, elucidate and clarify. With over 100 years of people interpreting Alexander's work, we perhaps understand the science and the teaching of it better than he.

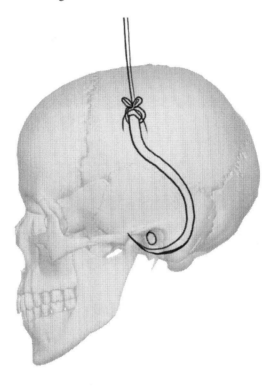

The revised "sky hook" image

One image that many of us have grown up with is that of "suspending" the headtop from the ceiling or sky. A more useful version of this sky hook image is to put the hook through the brainstem, the neural material between the ears. Then the head is not fixed and it can bobble.

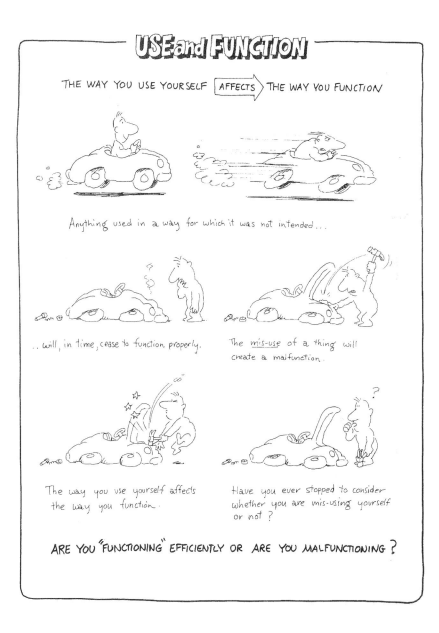

Use and Function cartoon from Direction Magazine

In the Alexander lessons shown in these two photos, the primary axis of the student moves as a single piece. Joan Murray, above, guides Gray Sutton into Alexander's hands on back of chair procedure with a deep, anthropoidal monkey. In the photo below, the primary axis maintains its integrity and can be imagined as a barrel that keeps its volume regardless of what happens with the legs. When the *whole barrel* is moved up off the legs, the legs are free to bend.

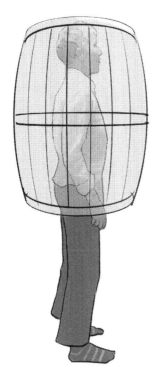
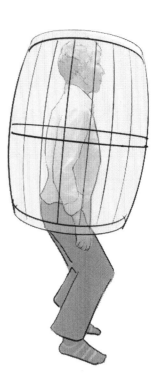

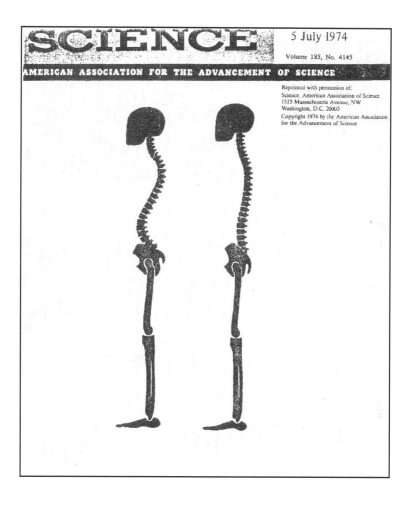

The **July 5, 1974 edition of Science magazine** featured the Nobel prize-winning speech of Nikolas Tinbergen and the recent publication of Dr. Wilfred Barlow's book, *The Alexander Principle*. Barlow was an MD who had been able to measure results of Alexander lessons during his service in WWII.

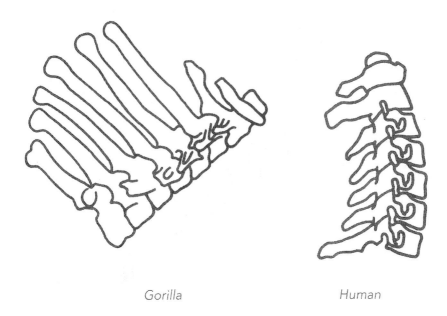

Gorilla   Human

Comparative spinous processes of primate neck vertebrae. Gorilla on left; human on right. From Phillip Tobias' *Man the Tottering Biped.*

The gorilla's spine is not vertical and therefore needs longer spinal attachments for the suboccipital muscles to counterbalance the weight of the head.

The much larger human head, however, evolved to be *poised* on top of a vertical spine, allowing the vertebral processes that hold the suboccipital muscles to shorten.

We all want to change, but most of us would like to be able to stay the same while we do so. We must give up what we know and step into the unfamiliar.

– Jeremy Chance

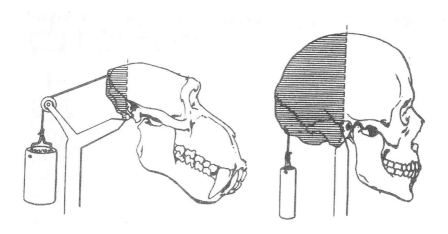

Skulls of baboon on the left, man on the right. Also from *Man the Tottering Biped*. Tobias' caption reads: "The suspended weights illustrate the difference in muscular bulk and strength required to hold the head on the vertebral column *in such a position that the eyes would have been able to look straight to the front.** In each instance the hatched part of the cranium is the proportion that lies behind the point of pivot on the spinal column. The tapering support shows the orientation of the spinal column and the position of its articulation with the cranium."

The amount and direction of pull of the suboccipital muscles changed with verticality as the much heavier human head became poised at the top of the spinal column.

The crux of the matter is to inhibit the immediate response of "trying to get it right" so that we have a chance to make a reasoned change. Seriously engaging in the process of change requires commitment, practice, and an ability to tolerate the unknown.

– Phyllis Richmond

*Italics are the author's.

More Examples of Bad Use

Unfortunate picture of the gracious Celine Dion distorting her primary axis to give a fan a close up. Note the boy's *use* is just fine.

Using a cane to support a slouch.

From the movie *Sling Blade*: Look at these two slumping.
No backs, no sit bones.

"You fellers seen 'Sling Blade,' I reckon."

***Sling Blade* cartoon,** *leading with the face:* The wiring for the face is at the top of the central nerve cord. In human evolution the face rotated 90° and became more three-dimensional. People who lead with their faces bend their central nerve cord 90° then pull their heads back to bring the brainpan and line of sight back to level.

145

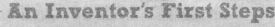

An Inventor's First Steps

While watching his granddaughters' soccer scrimmage, Jeffrey Nash, 60, spotted a mom helping her baby learn to walk. The father of three and grandfather of five had done this many times himself, but never noticed how awkward it was: the mom bending over and the child stumbling along.

Hence the inspiration for the Juppy Baby Walker, an infant harness with straps that can be held by Mom and Dad. Right away, he sketched a design and asked a tailor at the clothing store where he worked as a salesman to make a prototype. Using customers' kids to test it, he perfected the design, had a few hundred made, took time off from work, and began selling them out of his trunk. Nash, who was then 56 and divorced, quit his job of 15 years, cashed out his 401(k), sold his house at a loss, borrowed money from family and friends, secured a patent, created a website, and ordered 1,000 Juppys.

JEFFREY NASH
LAS VEGAS, NEV.

"I had never done anything like this before," he says. "But this was 2009, during the height of the recession. Companies were either laying off workers or hiring younger, less-expensive replacements, so I knew I had to do something."

So far, Nash estimates he's sold 35,000 Juppys worldwide through his website and wholesaler network. He's approaching $1 million in total revenue. "To work for a corporation is to be at its mercy," he says. "When viewed that way, it's really not a huge risk to start a business."

A route to bad backs.

How crazy is this? To think that you have to teach a child how to walk....

The following advertisements are a joke, a tongue-in-cheek nod to all of the quick fix proposals for improving one's *use*. (The fine print is not meant to be legible.) A recent *Time* magazine announced: "Microsoft made waves with its latest patent filing: electroshock clothing that jolts the wearer upright, ostensibly to correct bad posture." An *App* was developed in 2015 for the same purpose.

THE CHIP THAT STOPS YOUR SLOUCHING

LUMO LIFT / **$100**
AVAILABLE AT LUMOBODYTECH.COM

You can probably guess why so many people have posture that causes back pain: "We simply forget" to stop slouching, says Monisha Perkash, whose company, Lumo BodyTech, created the ultimate reminder. Once users clip the Lumo Lift, a chiplike gadget about the size of a thumb, onto their shirt, **it analyzes neck and spinal positions and vibrates when they're less than ideal.** Although the system isn't perfect—it can buzz when you lean for necessary reasons, like taking a phone call—it has exceeded internal sales goals. Half of its users are women, which is impressive given that early adopters for gadgets often tilt male.

POSTURE
PERFECT

Your mother probably repeated the stop-slouching refrain thousands of times. The Lumo Lift takes over where she (hopefully) left off: Gentle vibrations from a domino-size device attached via magnet to your shirt remind you to straighten up when you slump. The Lift also counts your daily steps and feeds that data (as well as your cumulative hours of good posture) to a companion smartphone app. $100; lumobodytech.com

4 | DECEMBER 29, 2014

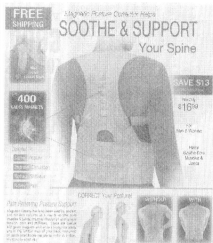

For Better or For Worse cartoon touts the physiological benefits of a smile.

The more that muscles are contracted, the less we are able to detect what the muscles and associated tissues and joints are doing. Contracted muscles decrease proprioceptive activity.

– David Garlick

This was a photo in a short article in Sports Illustrated in the early 1990s. The Denver Broncos' training camp uses the "Speed Chute" to train athletes in a way that keeps their backs back. Quarterback John Elway had a bad habit of pushing his lumbar spine forward, which, of course, shortened his mainstay, making his passing inconsistent. It is my opinion that the use of this device in training helped him lead the Broncos to two Super Bowl titles.

> Don't control the breathing, let the body
> do the breathing.
>
> – Kitty Wielopolska

Further Reading

Full bibliographical information is included only for books not listed in the bibliography.

Alexander's Four Books are not easy reading. The shortest and probably the easiest to read is *The Use of the Self*. The other three are: *Man's Supreme Inheritance (MSI), The Constructive Conscious Control of the Individual (CCCI)*, and *A Universal Constant in Living (UCL)*. The great American educator John Dewey wrote introductions to the first three and the physiologist George Coghill, to the fourth.

In 1992 *STAT Books* in London published an *Authorized Summary* of Alexander's four books, which had been commissioned by Alexander in the late 1940s in connection with the South African libel trial. Alexander initialed every page of the manuscript that was edited by Ron Brown, a veteran newspaper correspondent and editor as well as a student of the Alexander Technique. This book offers an excellent taste of Alexander's thinking.

FOR NEWCOMERS before EXPERIENCING ALEXANDER LESSONS:

Alexander Technique by Chris Stevens.

The Alexander Technique, a Skill for Life by Pedro de Alcantara. Crowood Press, Ltd. Wiltshire, UK. 1999.

The Alexander Technique, Joy in the Life of Your Body by Judith Stransky with Robert Stone, PhD. Beaufort Books, Inc. N.Y., 1981.

Back Trouble, A New Approach to Prevention and Recovery by Deborah Caplan. Her "emergency treatment series" is especially helpful.

Body Learning by Michael Gelb explains operational ideas and "learning how to learn." Great photos, especially in 1st & 2nd editions! In the back Gelb lists Alexander books and articles available up until 1981. This book complements *Your Natural Up*.

Fitness without Stress—A Guide to the Alexander Technique by Robert M. Rickover. Metamorphous Press. Portland, Or. 1988.

The Man Who Mastered Habit by Edward Owen, published in 1956 in London, was for many years available only as an inclusion in collected writings. It was recently republished as a pamphlet by Mornum Time Press. (Available through the American Society for the Alexander Technique, www.amsatonline.org.)

The Posturality of the Person—a Guide to Postural Education and Therapy by Ron Dennis, Ed.D. A good basic book, full of insights.

This book, *Your Natural Up*, gives an evolutionary understanding of the underlying conditions for *good use* and why *use* matters.

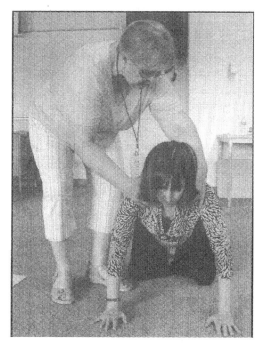

Rose Bronec helps Mara Sokolsky practice crawling

ONCE YOU'VE STARTED LESSONS

The Alexander Principle by Wilfred Barlow.

The Alexander Technique. J. Leibowitz & Bill Connington. Harper & Row, 1990.

How to Learn the Alexander Technique, a Manual for Students by Barbara Conable and Bill Conable.

Your Guide to the Alexander Technique by John Gray.

GETTING INTO IT DEEPER

Alexander Technique—The Essential Writings of F. M. Alexander edited by E. Maisel. Originally published in 1969 as *The Resurrection of the Body* by Dell Publishing Co.

Alexander Technique in Everyday Activity by Seán Carey. Hite Limited, London, 2015.

The Art of Changing, A New Approach to the Alexander Technique by Glen Park.

Body Awareness in Action by Frank Pierce Jones. Republished as *Freedom to Change*.

More Talk of Alexander by Wilfred Barlow.

ALEXANDER BIOGRAPHY

F.M. Alexander—The Life of Frederick Matthias Alexander by Michael Bloch.

PROFESSION AND OTHER SPECIALIZED BOOKS

Music
Indirect Procedures, a Musician's Guide to the Alexander Technique by Pedro de Alcantara. Clarendon Press, Oxford. 1997. Re-written second edition, Oxford University Press, 2013.

Inspiring Musical Performance by Ethan Kind. AmSAT News, Spring 2008. P.20-26.

The Integrated String Player by Pedro de Alcantara. In process as of June 2016. See pedrodealcantara.com/blog/ for exerpts and current information.

Mind and Muscle and Music by Elizabeth Langford. Alexandertechniek Centrum vzw. Leuven, 2008.

The Pianist's Talent by Harold Taylor. Kahn & Averill, London, 1979.

A Technique for Musicians by Frank Pierce Jones. A small pamphlet containing two articles written in 1949 and 1967. Available online at /http://www.alexandercenter.com/pa/musicjonesii.html.

Tensions in the Performance of Music edited by Carola Grindea. Kahn & Averill, London, 1978.

What Every Musician Needs to Know about the Body by Barbara Conable. Andover Press, Portland, OR, 2000.

Voice

Hints on Singing by Manuel Garcia. Joseph Patelson Music House, NY. Originally published in 1894. Several current editions available through amazon.com.

Voice and the Alexander Technique by Jane Ruby Heirich. Mornum Time Press. Berkeley, CA, 2005.

The Voice Book by Michael McCallion. Faber & Faber Ltd., London, 1989.

Acting and Theater

The Actor and The Alexander Technique by Kelly McEvenue. Palgrave Macmillan NY, 2002.

The Actor's Secret—Techniques for Transforming Habitual Patterns and Improving Performance by Betsy Polatin, 2013. Gets five stars from Amazon.

Movement for the Actor by Lucille S. Rubin. Drama Book Specialists, NY, 1980.

Physical Expression on Stage and Screen - Using the Alexander Technique to Create Unforgettable Performances by Bill Connington. Bloomsbury Publishing, London and New York, 2014.

Other

The Art of Swimming, a new direction using the Alexander Technique by Steven Shaw & Armand D'Angour. Ashgrove Publishing, London, 1996.

Be your self. Everyone else is already taken.

– Anonymous*

---

* Commonly attributed to Oscar Wilde. However, quoteinvestigator.com asserts that other possible authors are Thomas Merton and Gilbert Perreira.

Body Sense, Revolutionize your Riding with the Alexander Technique. [Horseback riding] by Sally A. Tottle. Trafalgar Square Publishing, Vermont, 1998.

Dance and the Alexander Technique—Exploring the Missing Link by Rebecca Nettl-Fiol and Luc Vanier. University of Illinois Press, Urbana, 2011.

Eyebody—The Art of Integrating Eye, Brain and Body by Peter Grunwald. Eyebody Press. Auckland, NZ, 2004.

Master the Art of Running, Raising your performance with the Alexander Technique by Malcolm Balk and Andrew Shields. Collins & Brown. London, 2006.

RELATED READING

The Anatomy Coloring Book by Lawrence M. Elson with Wynn Kapit.

Anatomy of Movement by Blandine Calais-Germain.

The Centered Skier by Denise McCluggage. Bantam Books, 1983.

Embrace Tiger, Return to Mountain, the essence of tai chi by Al Huang.

Expressive Movement — Posture and Action in Daily life, Sports and the Performing Arts by Pierce and Pierce.

The Hidden You by Mabel Elsworth Todd.

How you Stand, How you Move, How you Live—Learning the Alexander Technique by Missy Vineyard. Marlowe & Company, NY, 2007.

Material for the Spine DVD by Steve Paxton. Explorations of infant movement and other movement possibilities.

Mind body 40 Days by Sandra Bain Cushman. Robert Fripp, Spain, 2011.

Sensing, Feeling, and Action by Bonnie Bainbridge Cohen.

Understanding Balance, the Mechanics of Posture and Locomotion by Tristan D.M. Roberts, physiologist. Very scientific. Chapman & Hall, London, 1995.

Thinking influences what happens in your muscles.

– Kitty Wielopolska

Glossary

This glossary contains primarily anatomical and Alexander terms.

The Alexander Technique (AT) - Alexander called it "psychophysical re-education." The Alexander Technique is based upon the idea that how one *uses himself* affects how he functions and, over time, how he is structured. In practice, it's all about the back and our evolution as vertebrate animals. The "technique" of the Alexander Technique is in learning *NOT to do* one's habit of a lifetime, which has become almost reflexive.

Alexandroid - A stiff, robot-like carriage associated with trying to be "right" with one's *use*. Early Alexander experiences can leave students thinking that the work is about tucking their chins or straightening their necks, which they do in an attempt to replicate the feeling brought about by the Alexander lesson. An *Alexandroid* is trying to do something one can really only do by non-doing.

Awareness - Consciousness of how one is using his body in each and every moment. Consciousness of all the stimuli coming in from the outside world. "The basic awareness of one's internal and external world resides in the brainstem."[1]

AR - Albert Redden Alexander, FM's brother and one of his first apprentices. AR taught the Alexander Technique in Australia, London, and America.

Ashley Place - *16 Ashley Place*, Alexander's teaching studio in London where his teacher training courses met. "It was a small suite of rooms in a mansion block almost opposite Westminster Cathedral. It was dark and old-fashioned. When they weren't having class, AR would use the training course room as his teaching room."[2] FM maintained a private apartment in the basement. It was bombed during the Second World War (April 17, 1941) when the school was closed and FM was in America. After FM's death, Patrick Macdonald together with AR's son Max established a new training course there. Ashley Place was demolished in the early '70s.

Atlanto-occipital (AO) joint - Where the top vertebra (the atlas) articulates with the base of the skull. Where the head rests on the top of the spine.

Atlas - The top vertebra of the spine, which articulates with the head to allow the nod and which forms a pivot joint with second vertebrae, the *axis*, allowing the head to turn side to side.

Axis - Primary axis = sit bones to ears/occiput.
  Vertical axis = soles of feet to top of head.
Also, the second vertebrae of the spine—see *atlas*, above.

Back Back - The ancestral nerve cord is hardwired to be in the back of the body. It, in fact, defines the back—bones came much later. *Back back* is an Alexander *direction* purportedly coined by Patrick Macdonald.

Bilateral symmetry - Both sides are the same. Implies an elongated structure with a leading end, a front, and a back.

Bone is a tissue that is unique to vertebrates. "It is strong and hard, a composite of inorganic calcium phosphate mineral crystals plus organic collagen fibers. It first evolved as an external skeleton of the early fish, ostracoderms."[3]

Brainpan = the plane of the base of the skull. It likes to be level. On the exterior it can be inferred by palpating a line along the cheek bones to the hole in the ears and then the occiput. See *Frankfurt Horizontal.*

Brainstem - The ancestral brain. The earliest beginnings of a nerve center at the leading end of the dorsal nerve cord. In vertebrates, a continuation of the spinal cord that resides *inside the skull.* Like the rest of the spinal cord, the brainstem receives paired nerves, the *cranial nerves,* which service the specialized functions of the eyes, ears, nose, and face as well as autonomic functions outside the head like breathing and digestion. The hyphen-less spelling follows the lead of Frank Netter's 1989 edition of the *Atlas of Human Anatomy, Wikipedia,* and *Science News.* If a "primary control" can be located, this is where.

Caudal - Toward or pertaining to the tail.

Cephalization - The making of a head. In evolution, the gathering of the senses at the leading end.

Cephalo-caudal progression - Head to tail sequencing as exhibited in both development and movement. (Also, cranial-caudal)

Choice becomes possible when reflexive habits are inhibited.

Chakra - In the body there are seven chakras, energetic centers at critical turning points in the spine and inside the skull. *Chakra* is a sanskrit word for a wheel, disk, or circular organization.

Change - Alexander said: "Change involves carrying out an activity against the habits of a lifetime."

Contralateral movement is typical of human walking and running gaits. When one foot moves forward, the opposite arm and hand swing forward to create a spiral around the central axis and minimize side to side movement. Also called *heterolateral.* Another basic gait pattern is *homolateral,* with both limbs on one side moving forward at the same time and then both limbs on the other side. *Homologous* movement is typical of frogs, where the front limbs move together, then the hind limbs.

Cranial - Toward or pertaining to the head.

Cranial nerves - The twelve specialized pairs of "spinal nerves" that connect with the *brainstem*, the leading end of the primitive nerve cord inside the head. They connect with the sense organs, face, and tongue as well as autonomic functions outside the head like breathing and swallowing.

The Critical Moment - The moment when one's habit takes over (or not). The moment when we can inhibit a reflexive habit, creating the opportunity for re-programming. It is an opportunity for choice and change.

The Dart Procedures - A series of infantile movements, inspired by the work of South African anthropologist Raymond Dart, who had spent time on the floor with his developmentally challenged son, "rewiring him." Joan and Alex Murray, with encouragement from Dart, codified and completed the procedures to become an adjunct to Alexander's work, bringing more spirals to the AT and highlighting movement sequences through the body from head to foot.

Developmental movement - Progressive movement stages and patterns from embryo to toddler necessary for proper hardwiring as well as for the development of deep postural muscles.

Direction - In the AT, a set of orders suggesting the proper relationship of the parts of the body to each other in movement and at rest. Lengthening, widening, expanding multi-directionally. It always starts with "neck free."

> ***Neck free***. Head to move forward and up. Whole back to lengthen and widen. Widen into the upper arms. Knees forward and away. Back back.

> ***Forward*** refers to the relationship of the head to the neck/back. The head should fall forward from its point of balance at the top of the spine.

> ***Up*** is the direction that lengthens the segmented structure.

The ability **to *take direction*** is the ability to allow one's body to move with the suggestions of an Alexander teacher's hands or words. Marj Barstow said, "The individual I am working with has the responsibility of knowing that he or she is moving in the direction of the guidance my hands are giving them. The use of my hands is a direction to be followed."[4] Alexander would say, "altogether, one after the other."

End-gaining - Valuing the end over the means; being more concerned with the result than the process. Alexander discovered that if we are too invested in the end, we neglect the *means whereby*. End-gaining prevents us from being invested in the moment. To end-gain.

Entrainment - as in the head to tail (cephalocaudal) progression of muscle contraction. Once the lead muscles (the eyes) do something, the other muscles tend to do something organized around this lead muscle's action, rippling in a sequence.

Evodevo - Evolutionary developmental biology. Tiny changes in timing in a developing embryo can result in a vastly different adult animal. This *heterochrony* is the mechanism of evolution.

Fascia is the tough, responsive web of connective tissue that surrounds every muscle, bone, nerve fiber, and organ, holding the body together and stabilizing the body's tensegrity structure. "You would know if it were missing."[5] Colloquially, "sinew." "Over a lifetime fascia changes. In fact, some people say aging is connective tissue becoming tighter."[6]

FM - Frederick Matthias Alexander. Most of Alexander's friends and students called him this. His brother, Albert Redden, was referred to as "AR."

Foramen Magnum - The hole at the base of the skull through which the nerve cord passes. The ancestral nerve cord is now labeled to be divided into two parts: the spinal cord, outside the head, and the brainstem inside the skull.

Frankfurt Horizontal - "Internationally accepted baseline for the orientation of vertebrate skulls."[7] Officially a complicated measurement, but in practice, the *brainpan*, the horizontal line defined by the cheek bones, the hole in the ears, and the occiput. It puts the line of sight on the horizontal.

Habit - Habits can become reflexive. Alexander's specialty was the preparatory "sets" people would do in the moment before embarking upon an activity. Alexander said that "Habit need not be mindless. It should be plastic and creative."

Haeckel - Ernst Haeckel is known for "Haeckel's biogenetic law," the declaration that "Ontogeny recapitulates phylogeny." If translated correctly, it makes no sense—what Haeckel means is that ancestral developmental stages (rather than adult stages) are seen in modern embryonic development. The morphological comparisons in his 1874 chart, which appears in Chapter 1, are now backed up by genomics and molecular biology. (See also: *evodevo* in the glossary.)

Hardwiring in this book is used literally: the central nervous system of all elongate bilaterally symmetrical animals runs the length of the organism with the main controls at the head end. The central nervous system of all vertebrates runs down the back of the body

Hip bone (*the hips*) is a colloquial term for the two *innominate* bones, each a fusion of three gently curved bones that anchor the leg into the primary axis. The word, "pelvis" includes the bottom of the spine: the sacrum, to which the two wings of the hip bone are solidly glued, and the coccyx, the lowest part of the spine. In common American parlance, "hip bone" often refers to the prominent *iliac crest* in front.

Hox genes - The *homeobox complex of genes* are blueprints that establish position of body parts along the head to tail axis. This genetic toolkit is shared by the entire animal kingdom. The hox genes orchestrate the timing of master switches during development. They code for the protein, *sonic hedgehog*,* whose concentration affects the differentiation of the top of a segment from its bottom.

Inhibition - Alexander called it "the act of *refusing to respond* to some stimulus to psychophysical action." "The ability to stop/wait/pause before reacting to a stimulus." ("The mere thought of an activity is sufficient to enervate the muscles that habitually perform that activity."[8])

Innominate bone (*Os innominatum*) The hip bone(s). Each of the paired innominate bones is a fusion of three bones that anchor the legs into the primary axis. As the pelvic girdle, they form a stable ring at the pubis in front and with the sacrum in back. See also hip bone and pelvis.

Ischia - The sit bones, the ischial tuberosities. The lowest part of the pelvis. They function as rockers and support the primary axis in sitting.

---

* Sonic the Hedgehog is the name of a Japanese comic book character.

Kinaesthesia - Sensory appreciation. The sense of movement; the sense of the body's position in space and its relationship to gravity. Can become faulty (debauched) with chronic tension, emotional trauma, and *misuse*. *Debauched kinaesthesia* is now commonly referred to as "faulty sensory appreciation."

Kinesphere - The sphere of space surrounding a person.

The Main Beam, in this book, refers to the vertebrate central skeleton from the sit bones to the occiput. Architecturally a *beam* refers to a horizontal support (while a *post* is vertical). The main beam of vertebrate architecture evolved as a horizontal support and didn't discard that function as it evolved to vertical.

Means whereby - By staying present in each moment, inhibiting whatever needs to be inhibited, the end, will arrive. If you concern yourself with the present, the future will take care of itself. "Be here now."

Monkey - *A position of mechanical advantage* used by tennis player and fiddler alike. *Monkey* lowers the center of gravity thereby increasing stability. All six leg joints are flexed while the primary axis remains intact.

Neurulation - The formation of the nerve cord to create the first identifiable structure in the developing embryo.

Notochord - A flexible rod that holds a body's shape. In vertebrates it is apparent only embryonically, then morphs into the space-making discs of the spine.

Nuchal - Of or relating to the nape of the neck.

Pandiculation - The act of stretching and yawning, often referred to as the stretch-yawn syndrome (SYS), is the kind of stretching you do when you wake up.

Pelvic tilt – From semi-supine position: lifting the pelvis so that it no longer contacts the supporting surface. Can be large or small. Helps to engage the feet in semi-supine.

Pelvis - Latin for basin. The sacrum is glued into the wings of the hip bones in back to form the pelvis with the coccyx curving around the bottom to form a bowl. The two halves of the "hip bone" are the *innominate* bones, each a fusion of three gently curved bones that anchor the legs into the primary axis and form a stable ring, the *pelvic girdle*, for the whole container. The sacrum is the keystone of the pelvic arch.

Pentapodal = five feet. *Pentapodal position* has five weight-bearing points, the arms, legs, and the head. Also "prayer position" and "kowtow."

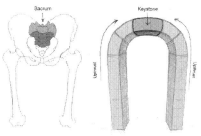

Posture should be considered as "the sum total of the positions and movements of the body throughout the day and throughout life."[9]

Primary Control – Among Alexander teachers there is discrepancy about what we mean by "primary control," a term coined by animal physiologist Rudolf Magnus in 1924 after Alexander had been teaching his work for thirty years. Alexander started using the term, which he considered to be "the relationship of the head to the neck/back" (*the head/neck/back or HNB* relationship) that affected the functioning of the entire organism. He had espoused the belief that this relationship was a "central control" that should be "a true and primary movement in each and every activity."

Magnus had demonstrated in his work with salamanders that the postural reflexes were integrated at the anatomical center of the brainstem. "There is an underlying mechanism within the brainstem which acts as a primary control. Posture is consequently influenced by the position of the head, where the head leads and the body follows."[10]

The "total pattern" of the HNB dominates all partial patterns of the limbs. The brainstem is the coordination center for all action; it functions best when its well-being is secure, remaining in back, in line with the rest of the nerve cord.

Proprioception - The self perception of everything within one's body. The sense of the relationship of the parts of the body to each other: how the hand knows where the mouth is or where to scratch an itch. Proprioception includes visceral perceptions.

Psychophysical re-education - The Alexander Technique, for example.

Red and white muscles - The muscles next to the bones, red in color, are "slow-twitch" and don't tire easily—they're indefatigable. These are the deep postural muscles that stabilize the bones so that they can conduct upthrust. They are strengthened for upright activity through the infantile movements of wriggling, rolling, creeping, and crawling. The peripheral muscles, white in color, are "fast twitch" and are made for activity, running, lifting. They DO tire.

Attitudinal Reflexes

[The German physiologist Rudolf] "Magnus found in his experiments that there was a *central mechanism* [the *primary control*] which automatically controlled a large number of reflexes. This central mechanism was activated by placing the head in different positions. The effect on the whole animal was a change in the distribution of muscle tonus throughout the whole body. This change of muscle tonus brought about a change in the position of different parts of the body relative to others, a different attitude. This is the reason why these reflexes are called *attitudinal reflexes*; every change in position of the head is followed immediately by the corresponding change in attitude of the whole body. The attitudinal reflexes are evoked by changing the position of the head either in space (the vestibular mechanism) or in relation to the body (proprioceptive messages from the suboccipitals). These reflexes are called *tonic* and last as long as the head stays in a certain position. They are practically indefatigable."[11]

Righting reflex - The reflex to keep one's head upright and level, which automatically and sequentially brings the body into line.

Stretch Reflex - A stretch reflex is the automatic contraction of a muscle in response to being stretched. In standing it starts in the feet, which must be allowed to spread in order to activate the muscles that elastically hold us up. The stretch reflexes inform the central mechanism about how and where weight is falling and are likely to be the basis for muscle action.

Startle Pattern is a reflex that retracts the head, raises the shoulders, flattens the chest, straightens the arms and bends the legs. It changes the balance of the head, pulling the neck forward while pulling the head back and down, affecting the function of all reflexes. Raymond Dart referred to it as a prototypical response to fear.[12] Scientists conjecture that in this age of constant stimulus, we never have a chance to recover from our recent "encounter with a saber toothed tiger." The posture of the startle reflex seems to become the norm for many people as they age.

Semi-Supine - A position of mechanical advantage. Lying on one's back with knees up and soles of feet touching the floor. Most people will need an inch or two of books to support their heads. There are thirteen points of bony contact and support: three on each foot, the back of hips, shoulders, elbows on each side, and the back of the head. Because you can't fall off the floor, semi-supine creates an opportunity to do nothing, to cease all muscular activity. It uses the floor and gravity to help define the plane of the back.

Sit bones - Also, *sitz bones*, *sitting bones*, and *ischial tuberosities*. The lowest part of the pelvis evolved to conduct upthrust from a surface through the primary axis in sitting. The sit bones function as rockers; they point in a direction opposite that of the head.

Sitting Tripod - A position of mechanical advantage. Two sit bones plus one tripod of each foot. (This is, in fact, a trapezoid.)

Small Dance - the small adjustments we make to maintain our balance in verticality. A latent dance with gravity within each of us. In the art/sport dance form *contact improvisation* one learns to play with the edges of balance from positions other than standing; partners find a shared *small dance* to initiate falling or other momentum-generating movement.

Somites - Embryonic blocks of presumptive material flanking the nerve cord. The embryos of most bilaterally symmetrical animals show the segmentation of somites in early development. Each somite will morph into a specific pre-determined destiny. In reptiles the material that is to become the first two vertebrae will be recruited to form the bone of the occiput in mammals.

It's not a position, it's a movement.

– Marj Barstow

Suboccipital muscles - Between the back of the head and the neck. Function as a tensile counterbalance to the weight of the head. Nerves embedded in these muscles provide information to the balance organs. "The handmaids of the cranial globe."[13]

Tan-t'ian (or *dantian*) - Chinese term referring to the body's center of gravity, approximately two inches below navel and two/thirds of the way back. *Hara* in Japanese, which translates as "belly."

Tensegrity - In human bodies, the idea of bones as spacers elastically supported by connective tissue. Bodies get their strength and integrity from their space.* Think suspension bridges, jello, or balloons, which have both firmness and give.

Tension - Not slack. Overly tense muscles will not let the weight of the bones hang. Nerves from chronically tense muscles cease to relay accurate information, which leads to debauched kinaesthesia. In physics the opposite of tension is weight—when muscles aren't holding, weight can hang.

Upthrust – Gravity's equal but opposite force. An architectural term. While gravity acts upon every individual molecule, upthrust acts only through contact. Awareness of one's contact with the ground (and trusting it) allows upthrust to support the skeletal structure.

Urbilateria - the conjectured ancestor of all bilaterally symmetrical animals. The separation of the vertebrates from the insects and worms happened as early as 700-800 million years ago, some 300 million years before the Cambrian explosion. All animals share the same genetic toolkit.

Use - "The *use* of the self." *Use* affects function and, over time, structure. Character is expressed by *use*. *Poor use* has many origins including premature walking (social and/or psychological pressure to walk too soon), imitation (usually of one's parent), peer group pressure (the teenage slouch, the modeling industry), physical or emotional trauma internalized in musculature/structure and now chronic, the stresses of modern society, and the chair. According to Alexander teacher, Robert Rickover, the term 'use' was borrowed from the language of horse trainers.[15]

Vestibular - referring to balance. The primary organs of balance are in the inner ear, just above the atlanto-occipital joint.

---

* Sample definitions of tensegrity in Buckminster Fuller's *Synergetics*[14] include: Pneumatic structures. geodesics, simple curvature=the barrel. Sphericity and spherical/triangular unity. Sample subtitles in that chapter: Three-way great circling; gravity as a circumferential force; struts as chords in a spherical network. The clothesline. Masts. Miniaturization. Balloons, snow mound. Discontinuous compression, convergence, Allspace Filling. Eternality. Moebius Strip and Klein Bottle. Allspace-filling tensegrity arrays.

Think a smile.

Whispered Ah - A vocal exercise that helps organize the relationships of the jaw to the skull and the jaw/skull to the neck/back. The *whispered ah* reinforces the sense of one's brainpan.

Keep the neck free, refusing to tighten the neck at every moment. The *whispered ah* starts with a smile, or, rather, thinking a smile. (Without tightening the lips, grin with your lips together and teeth apart.) The exercise begins with an exhalation—as you make an aspirated "ah" sound, the jaw will project forward while dropping down. Leave your tongue on the floor of mouth with its tip touching the back of the lower teeth. The neck must remain free of tension.

I call it the penthouse.

– Rivka Cohen

A Note on the Verbiage of Anatomical Relationship

The word *anterior* defines us with respect to our environment, but not ourselves. The anterior end of a horse is his head; but for us humans, now vertical, anterior is our face/stomach (ventral). What was anterior for our embryo is now "headward" (cranial). How soon after birth does anterior become "headward? In teaching, I use "toward the crown chakra or the top of the head."

A Note on Worldwide Alexander Associations and Affiliations

STAT - The Society of Teachers of the Alexander Technique headquartered in London is the mother organization. It was formed just a few years after Alexander's death to establish standards for teaching and training (1600 hours).

ATAS - Alexander Technique Affiliated Societies. As of 2016, the seventeen STAT-affiliated organizations represent Australia, Austria, Belgium, Brazil, Canada, Denmark, Finland, France, Germany, Israel, The Netherlands, New Zealand, Norway, South Africa, Spain, Switzerland, and the United States. Among other countries with STAT-accredited teachers are Argentina, China, Colombia, Cyprus, Estonia, Greece, Hungary, India, Iran, Ireland, Italy, Japan, Mexico, Poland, Romania, Sweden, Taiwan, and Uruguay. See: www.alexandertechniqueworldwide.com.

AmSAT, The American Society for the Alexander Technique, is the US's official affiliate to STAT.

ACAT - The American Center for the Alexander Technique, was established in New York in the mid 1960s before any STAT-affiliated societies existed. It survives and thrives as a center for promoting the work.

ATI is an independent international organization that was formed by Alexander teachers who were apprenticed by Marj Barstow (who, at the time, denied that she was apprenticing anybody). Its affiliate schools, with their own training standards, produce highly qualified teachers who tend to eschew Alexander's "procedures."

What happens if you contract every muscle of your body?
You stop breathing and you get smaller. So get big again;
get as big as you can allow yourself to be.

– Marion Rosen

Endnotes by Chapter

Introduction

1. **The right *use* of one's body:** Lulie Westfeldt quoting friend Kitty Wielopolska in *F. Matthias Alexander: The Man and his Work* (California, 1986), p.28.

2. **In small and unobtrusive ways:** Wilfred Barlow, *The Alexander Principle* (London, 1991), p.128.

Chapter 2, Verticality

1. **All major groups of non-human primates:** Phillip V. Tobias, *Man, the Tottering Biped—The Evolution of his Posture, Poise and Skill* (New South Wales, 1982) p.12, quoting Poirier.

2. **The legs just tag along:** Marj Barstow from the author's personal notes.

Chapter 4, Alexander

1. **The [mere] thought of an activity:** Jack Fenton, *Practical Movement Control* (London, 1973) p.8. Fenton's exact quote is: "The thought of an action is sufficient to enervate the muscles which habitually perform it," which closely resembles (with no acknowledgement) Eric de Peyer's words on page 4 of his 1948 pamphlet *Posture, Habit and Health*. De Peyer said, "It has been shown by electric recording instruments that even the *thought* of an action is sufficient to activate the muscles which habitually perform it." Fenton's quote, with the addition of "mere" appears twice in the text of this book.

2. **The way the head is oriented:** Patrick Macdonald, *The Alexander Technique as I See It* (England, 1989), p.40.

3. **One of changing and controlling:** Source unknown.

4. **He encouraged his students:** Marjory Barlow, *Alexander Technique: The Ground Rules—in conversation with Sean Carey* (London, 2011), p.65.

5. (in footnote) **He considered the whole idea:** Michael Bloch, *F.M. Alexander—The Life of Frederick Matthias Alexander, Founder of the Alexander Technique* (London, 2004), p.143.

6. **This is all going to die with you:** M. Barlow, p.70.

7. (in footnote) **When he realized:** Westfeldt, p.76; Bloch, p.233.

8. **There are more teachers:** Westfeldt, p.100.

9. **The Alexander Technique bears the same relationship:** John Dewey in the introduction to Alexander's *The Use of the Self* (London, 1943), p.xix.

Chapter 5, Taking a Lesson

1. **Alexander teacher Bruce Fertman says:** Marj Barstow workshop summer 1977, Lincoln, NE.

2. **Further light was shed on my *use* of myself:** Frank Pierce Jones, "A New Field for Inquiry." Jones' account of his first AT lessons with Alexander's brother, A.R. *Collected Writings on the Alexander Technique.* (Chicago, 1948), p.2.

3. **Physiological benefits include:** Michael Protzel, editor, *Kinesthetic Ventures Informed by the Work of F.M Alexander, Stanislavski, Pierce & Freud* by Ed Bouchard and Ben Wright, (Chicago, 1997), p.35.

4. **The new aches and pains still go on:** Louise Morgan, *Inside Yourself,* (London, 1954), p.25.

Chapter 6, The Use of the Self

1. **Alexander realized that the choices:** Gelb, p.11.

2. **Standing folded:** Ann Matthews gets credit for this logical terminology.

3. (in footnote) **Explained by the dehydration:** David Garlic, "The Garlic Report," *Direction V.2 #2,* (1994), p.5.

4. **The three gangly youths:** Gelb, p.125. Gelb capitalizes "Use" throughout his book.

5. **If we try to hold on to well-aligned balance:** David Gorman, *Looking at Ourselves, Articles, Lectures, and Columns 1984-1996. Thinking about Thinking about Ourselves* (London, 1997), p.9.

6. **It is as if each of us is trying:** Marjory Barlow, 1965 Alexander Memorial Lecture: "The Teaching of F. Matthias Alexander." Reprinted in *More Talk of Alexander—Aspects of the Alexander Technique* (London, 1978), p.17.

7. **As the elderly:** Source unknown.

Chapter 7, Tensegrity

1. (In footnote) **The term tensegrity:** Thomas W. Myers, *Anatomy Trains* (London, 2001), p.42.

2. **Float in a sea of continuous tension:** Myers, p.44.

3. **The connective tissue will always:** Gorman, *Looking at Ourselves, Talented Tissues.* p.35.

4. **It reacts and remembers:** Christopher McDougall, *Natural Born Heroes: How a Daring Band of Misfits Mastered the Lost Secrets of Strength and Endurance* (New York, 2015), p.72.

5. **Over time fascial structure will accommodate posture:** Myers, p.33.

6. **Without the soft tissues:** Myers, p.45.

7. **The true and primary movement:** FM Alexander. common knowledge. (He didn't call it the "main beam.")

8. **The spine is a series:** Gorman, *Thinking about Thinking about Ourselves,* p.9.

9. **God designed the shoulder girdle:** Conable from author's notes

10. **Humans are amazing throwers:** McDougall, pp. 74 & 75.

11. **They lose the ability:** David Garlic @ 2nd International Congress in Brighton, England. 1988.

12. **Red muscle likes rhythmic movement:** Ibid.

13. **If the stretch reflex network:** Ted Dimon, "The Organization of Movement, Four Talks on the Primary Control," *AmSAT Journal Spring 2013-Fall 2014*, p.19.

14. **This involuntary feedback loop:** Gorman, *Looking at Ourselves, Talented Tissues*, p.37.

15. **Instead of thinking:** Gorman, *Thinking about Thinking about Ourselves*, p.6.

16. **Instead of trying to hold ourselves up:** Ibid, p.9.

17. **The body is a suspension system:** Gorman, *Looking at Ourselves, The Suspension System*, p.46.

18. **Our inherent instability:** Gorman, *Looking at Ourselves, Talented Tissues*, p.33.

19. **Equilibrium is a dynamic and ongoing:** Gorman, *Looking at Ourselves, More Suspense*, p.54.

Chapter 8, Lifetime Habits

1. **Do a teeny wilt, then lengthen out of it:** Ron Dennis, Ed.D., *The Posturality of the Person—a Guide to Postural Education and Therapy*. Posturality Press. (Atlanta, GA, 2013) p.29.

2. **It is the choices we make:** Gelb, p.137.

Appendix 1, Quotes

1. **As we grow up:** Janet O'Brien Stillwell, "Interview with Marjorie L. Barstow," *Somatics*, 1981. p.17.

2. **Belief is a certain standard:** FM Alexander, 1934 "Bedford Lecture." at Bedford Physical Training College, 8/3/34. Printed in *F. Matthias Alexander Articles and Lectures* (London, 1995) p.174. "Belief is a matter of customary muscle tension," according to Lulie Westfeldt, is how he first voiced it.

3. **I am not interested:** Westfeldt, p.68.

4. **If we become sensorily aware:** Ibid, p.71.

5. **I never stop working on myself:** M. Barlow, "1965 Alexander Memorial Lecture," p.28.

6. **Of course *directions* are doings:** Shoshana Kaminitz, "Mr. Macdonald," *Direction V.2, #5*, (1994), p.7.

7. **When there is an interference:** Stillwell, p.16.

8. **The suboccipital muscles are:** Gitte Dollerup Fjordbo, *On the Development of Habit*. (Denmark, 1992), p.36. quoting A. Murdoch: "The suboccipital muscles together with the top two vertebrae = the handmaids of the cranial globe."

9. **If you react straight away:** Frances Oxford, "Marjorie Barstow Interviewed," *Direction V2, #2*, (1994), p.18.

10. **One thing you can do:** Ibid.

11. **Dilys Carrington quotes:** Nicholls, Lynn. *Dilys Carrington as interpreted by Lynn Nicholls.* n.a.

12. **I really think I prefer:** Anthony Spawforth, *Taking Time* edited by Chariclia Gounaris (Denmark, 2000), p.102.

13. **Eric de Peyer quotes:** de Peyer, *Posture, Habit and Health,* (Isobel Cripps Centre, UK. No date). First quote, page 4.

14. **What you think is what you get:** Fiona Robb, *Not To Do* (London, 1999), p.94.

15. **Aim up and stay back:** Rivka Cohen "The Primary Control: Some Personal Views." *AmSAT News #46,* (2000), p.9.

16. *Direction* **has the two meanings of:** Macdonald, p.4.

17. **The Alexander Technique is interested in:** Ibid, p.5

18. **I can teach you to do this, but I can't learn you.** Ibid, p.11

19. **Alexander understood Reich's theory that:** Kitty Wielopolska, *Never Ask Why* (Denmark, 2001), p.134.

20. **The ground activates the reflexes to go up:** Cohen, "The Primary Control," *AmSAT News #46,* (2000), p.9.

21. **Are you ready for anything:** Pedro de Alcantara, "Whack! Smack! Ka-POW! Teaching Alexander Technique as a Martial Art," *AmSAT News #77,* 2008, p.23.

22. **As I see it, to direct is to sense:** Ibid.

23. **The F. Matthias Alexander Technique is:** John Coffin, "Review on 'The Collected Writings on the Alexander Technique,'" *Direction Journal* #8, July 2000. P. 5 of insert.

24. **Even snakes yawn:** Author's notes.

25. **Instead of thinking of gravity's downward pull:** Gorman, *Thinking about Thinking about Ourselves,* p.6.

26. **The joints of the spine are distortion joints:** Ibid, p.9.

27. *Inhibition* **is implicit in** *direction:* Eleanor Rosenthal, "Judith Liebowitz: Her Legacy." *The Congress Papers, Engelberg, Switzerland* (1991), p. 28.

28. **The head is poised, not positioned.** Liebowitz, "The Alexander Technique," *AmSAT Journal #3,* (2013), p.41.

29. **Life is in one sense body mechanics:** Ann Mathews, "Ann Sickels Mathews in Her Own Words" with Elizabeth Huebner and Phyllis G. Richmond. *AmSAT News* (Winter 2007), p.23.

30. **If someone has gone around for 35 years:** John Nicholls, *The Alexander Technique, In Conversation with John Nicholls and Sean Carey,* UK, 1991, pp. 62 & 63.

31. **The crux of the matter is:** Phyllis Richmond, "The Alexander Technique and Dance." *The Alexander Journal #11* (Spring 1991), p.23.

32. **We tend to think we know:** Ibid, p.22

33. **You are learning to take advantage of:** Editor Phyllis Richmond's note paraphrasing summary of Dr. Chris Stevens' article, "New Developments in the Alexander Technique," *AmSAT News #64,* p.25.

34. **The postural system has widespread links:** Dr. Christopher H.H. Stevens, "New Developments in the Alexander Technique," *AmSAT News #64*, p.24.

35. **As the animal grows:** Coghill via Barlow in "The Mind body Relationship." Author's notes.

36. **In human beings the head moves:** Raymond Dart, "The Attainment of Poise." *South African Medical Journal*, (Feb. 8, 1947), p.90; reprinted in *Skill and Poise*, p.149.

37. **The basic discovery Alexander made:** Dart, *An Anatomist's Tribute to the Alexander Technique*. Reprinted in *Skill and Poise*, p.19.

38. **As Mr. Alexander points out:** John Dewey, in introduction to Alexander's *The Use of the Self*, p.xvi.

39. **It became apparent to me:** Macdonald, quoting McDonaugh, p.89.

40. **Sherrington quotes:** Sir Charles Sherrington, "The Brain and its Mechanism." Cambridge University Press, 1937, via *The Alexander Journal #7* (Spring 1972), p.30.

41. **If you feel that the teacher:** Kaminitz "Mr. Macdonald,"p.8; quoting from "The Hundred Verses of the Spear."

42. **If it weren't for time:** Source unknown.

43. **A means to free ourselves from:** Magnus via Gelb, p.49.

44. **A method for keeping:** Leo Stein via Frank Pierce Jones in *Body Awareness in Action*, p.48.

Appendix 4, Glossary

1. **The basic awareness:** Bruce Bower, "Consciousness in the Raw, The Brainstem May Orchestrate the Basics of Awareness," *Science News* (Sept. 15, 2007).

2. **It was a small suite of rooms:** M. Barlow, *The Ground Rules*, p.51.

3. **It is strong and hard:** Leonard B. Radinsky, *The Evolution of Vertebrate Design*, (University of Chicago Press, 1987) p.39.

4. **The individual I am working with:** William Brenner, "Practical Marj," *Austat Journal, Vol.1, #2*, p.31.

5. **You would know if it were missing:** Bill Hayes, *The Anatomist*, quoting Charlie Ordahl, Bellevue Literary Press, (NY, 2009) p.173.

6. **Over a lifetime fascia changes:** Ibid.

7. **Internationally accepted baseline:** Tobias, p.30 in footnote.

8. **The mere thought of an activity:** de Peyer.

9. **Posture should be considered:** Beckett Howorth, M.D. "Dynamic Posture," *Journal of the American Medical Association*, 8/24/46. Via Ron Dennis Ed.D, *The Posturality of the Person*, p.44.

10. **There is an underlying mechanism:** Rudolf Magnus, *Körperstellung* in 1924.

11. **Magnus found in his experiments:** Fjordbo, pp. 33 & 34.

12. **Raymond Dart referred to it as:** Gelb, p.52.

13. **The handmaids of the cranial globe:** M. Barlow, Marjory. Author's notes. (Attributed to A. Murdoch.)

14. (in footnote) **Sample definitions of tensegrity:** Buckminster Fuller, *Synergetics* (New York, 1975), pp. 370-371.

15. **The term "use" was borrowed from the language of horse trainers:** Robert Rickover, "Viewpoint." *Direction V.2, #5* (1994), p.34.

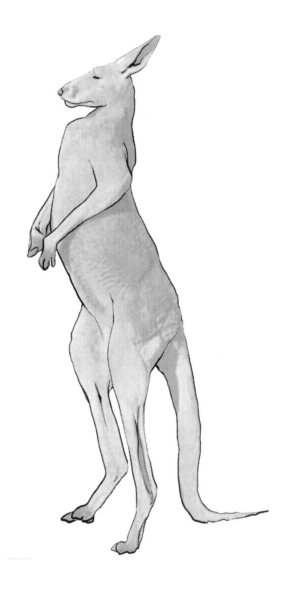

Bibliography and References

Books

Alexander, FM. *The Constructive Conscious Control of the Individual.* Chaterson Ltd., London, 1923.

Alexander, FM. *Man's Supreme Inheritance.* Chaterson Ltd., London, 1946. First published, 1910; revised, 1918.

Alexander, FM. A Universal Constant in Living. E.P. Dutton & Co., Inc., New York, 1941.

Alexander, FM. *The Use of the Self.* Chaterson Ltd, London 1943. First published, 1932.

Alexander, FM. *F. Matthias Alexander Articles and Lectures.* Compiled by Jean M.OI. Fischer and Mouritz, London, 1995.

Arey, Leslie Brainerd. *Developmental Anatomy.* W.B. Saunders Co., Philadelphia, 1966.

Armstrong, Joe. *Never Ask Why, The Life-Adventure of Kitty Wielopolska as told to Joe Armstrong.* Novis Publications, Denmark, 2001.

Balinsky, B.I. *Introduction to Embryology.* W.B. Saunders Co. Philadelphia, 1969.

Barlow, Marjory. *Alexander Technique: The Ground Rules—in conversation with Sean Carey.* HITE Ltd., London, 2011.

Barlow, Wilfred. *The Alexander Principle.* Victor Gollancz ltd., London, 1991. First published, 1973.

Barlow, Wilfred, editor. *More Talk of Alexander—Aspects of the Alexander Technique.* Mouritz, London, 1978.

Binkley, Goddard. *The Expanding Self.* STAT Books, London, 1993.

Bloch, Michael. *F.M. Alexander. The Life of Frederick Matthias Alexander, Founder of the Alexander Technique.* Little Brown, London, 2004.

Bouchard, Ed and Ben Wright. *Kinesthetic Ventures Informed by the Work of F.M Alexander, Stanislavski, Pierce & Freud.* Edited by Michael Protzel. Mesa Press, Chicago, 1997.

Bowden, George C. *F. Matthias Alexander and the Creative Advance of the Individual.* L.N. Fowler & Co. Ltd., London, 1965.

Bromley, Lyn Ph.D. *Monkeys, Apes & Other Primates.* Bellerophon Books, California, 1981.

Brown, Richard A. with Lester Thompson. *The Scientific and Humanistic Contributions of Frank Pierce Jones on the F. Matthias Alexander Technique.* Based on papers presented at the first International Congress in 1986. Centerline Press, California, 1988.

Calais-Germain, Blandine. *Anatomy of Movement.* Eastland Press, Seattle, 1993.

Caplan, Deborah. *Back Trouble A New Approach to Prevention and Recovery.* Triad Publishing Company, Gainesville, Fla., 1987.

Carey, Sean. *The Alexander Technique in Conversation with John Nicholls and Sean Carey.* Redwood Press Limited, UK, 1991.

Carrington, Walter. *Walter Carrington on the Alexander Technique in discussion with Sean Carey.* Shieldrake Press, London, 1986.

Carrington, Walter. *Personally Speaking. Walter Carrington with Sean Carey.* Shieldrake Press, London, 1986.

Carroll, Sean B. *Endless Forms Most Beautiful—The New Science of Evo Devo.* W.W. Norton & Company, NY, 2005

Charlip, Remy. *First Remy Charlip Reader.* Contact Editions, Northampton, MA, 1986.

Cockrum, E. Lendell and William J. McCauley. *Zoology.* W.B. Saunders Co., Philadelphia, 1965.

Cohen, Bonnie Bainbridge & Margret Mills. *Developmental Movement Therapy.* Self published, Amherst, MA, 1979.

Cohen, Bonnie Bainbridge. *Ontogenetic and Phylogenetic Developmental Principles.* School for Body/Mind Centering, 1977.

Cohen, Bonnie Bainbridge. *Sensing, Feeling and Action.* Contact Editions, Northampton, MA, 1993

Coyle, Terence and Robert Beverly Hale, editors. *Albinus on Anatomy.* Dover, NY, 1979.

Conable, Barbara. *How to Learn the Alexander Technique, a Manual for Students.* Andover Road Press, Columbus, Ohio, 1995.

Conable, Barbara, editor. *Marjorie Barstow, Her Teaching and Training.* Andover Road Press, Columbus, Ohio, 1989.

Dart, Raymond. *Skill, Poise, and the Alexander Technique.* Centerline Press. Four papers from 1946-70.

Darwin, Charles. *The Expression of the Emotions in Man and Animals.* University of Chicago Press, Chicago, 1965.

de Alcantara, Pedro. *Indirect Procedures.* Oxford University Press, New York, 2013.

Dennis, Ron.Ed.D. *The Posturality of the Person—a Guide to Postural Education and Therapy.* Posturality Press, Atlanta, GA, 2013.

Dimon, Theodore. *The Body in Motion—Its Evolution and Design.* North Atlantic Books, Berkeley, CA, 2011.

Elson, Lawrence M. with Wynn Kapit. *The Anatomy Coloring Book*. Harper & Collins, New York, 1993.

England, Marjory A. with George Matsumura. *Embryology Coloring Book*. Wolf Publishing, Barcelona, 1992.

Evans, J.A. *Frederick Matthias Alexander, A Family History*. Phillimore & Co. Ltd., London, 2001.

Fenton, Jack Vinten. *Practical Movement Control*. Plays, Inc., Great Britain, 1973.

Fisher, Jean M.O., ed. *Aphorisms*. Mouritz, London, 2000.

Fischer, Jean M.O., editor. *The Philosopher's Stone. Diaries of Lessons with F. Matthias Alexander*. Mouritz, London, 1998.

Fjordbo, Gitte Dollerup. *On the Development of Habit*. Hvalso, Denmark, 1992.

Fuller, Buckminster. *Synergetics*. MacMillan Pub. Co., NY, NY, 1975.

Garlic, David. *The Lost Sixth Sense*. University of New South Wales Press, NSW, 1980.

Garlic, David. *Proprioception, Posture and Emotion*. Adept Printing, Bankstown, NSW, 1982.

Gelb, Michael. *Body Learning*. Henry Holt & Co., New York, 1987.

Goldberg, Marian, editor. *Beginning from the Beginning. The Growth of Understanding and Skill*. Marian Goldberg, 1996.

Gorman, David. *The Body Moveable. Vol.I, The Trunk & the Head* and *Vol.III, The Lower Limb*. Ampersand Printing Co., Ontario, CA, 1981.

Gorman, David. *Looking at Ourselves, Articles, Lectures, and Columns 1984-1996*. Learning Methods, London, 1997.

Gould, Steven J. *A Wonderful Life, The Burgess Shale and the Nature of History*. W.W. Norton & Co., NY, NY, 1989.

Gounaris, Chariclia, editor. *Taking Time*. Interviews by Crissman Taylor and Carmen Tarnowski. Novis, Denmark, 2000.

Gray, Henry S. *Gray's Anatomy*. Bounty Books, NY, 1977. First published in 1858. Illustrated by Henry Vandyke Carter.

Gray, John. *Your Guide to the Alexander Technique*. Victor Gollancz Ltd., London, 1990.

Hale, Robert Beverly and Terence Coyle, editors. *Albinus on Anatomy*. Dover, NY, 1979.

Hayes, Bill. *The Anatomist: A True Story of Gray's Anatomy*. Bellevue Literary Press, NY, 2009.

Huang, Al Chung Liang. *Embrace Tiger, Return to Mountain, the Essence of Tai Chi*. Real People Press, Moab, Utah, 1973.

Jones, Frank Pierce. *Body Awareness in Action*. Schocken Books, NY, 1976. (Re-published as *Freedom to Change*.)

Kapit, Wynn with Lawrence Elson. *The Anatomy Coloring Book.* Harper & Collins, New York, 1993.

Larsen, William J. *Human Embryology.* Churchill Livingstone, Inc., NY, NY, 1993.

Macdonald, Patrick. *The Alexander Technique as I See It.* Rahula Books, Brighton, England, 1989.

McNamara, Kenneth J. *Shapes of Time, the Evolution of Growth and Development.* Johns Hopkins University Press, Baltimore, 1997.

Matsumura, George with Marjory A. England. *Embryology Coloring Book.* Wolf Publishing, Barcelona, 1992.

Matt, Pamela. *A Kinesthetic Legacy. The Life and Works of Barbara Clark.* CMT Press, Tempe, AZ, 1993.

McCauley, William J. and E. Lendell Cockrum. *Zoology.* W.B. Saunders Co., Philadelphia, 1965.

McDougall, Christopher. *Born to Run.* Alfred A. Knopf, New York, 2009.

McDougall, Christopher. *Natural Born Heroes: How a Daring Band of Misfits Mastered the Lost Secrets of Strength and Endurance.* Knopf, New York, 2015.

McNamara, Kenneth J. *Shapes of Time—The Evolution of Growth and Development.* Johns Hopkins University Press, Baltimore, 1997.

Mees, L.F.C. *Secrets of the Skeleton—Form in Metamorphosis.* Anthroposophic Press, Spring Valley, NY, 1984.

Mills, Margret & Bonnie Bainbridge Cohen. *Developmental Movement Therapy.* Self published, Amherst, MA, 1979.

Miranda, Kathryn. *Dare to Be Wrong, the Teaching of Judith Leibowitz.* ACAT, New York, 2007.

Morgan, Louise. *Inside Yourself.* Anchor Press, Ltd., London, 1954.

Murray, Alexander Douglass. *F.M. Alexander in his Own Words, and in the Words of Those Who Knew Him.* Murray, Alexander D., 2011.

Myers, Thomas W. *Anatomy Trains.* Churchill Livingstone, London, 2001.

Nelken, Shmuel. *The Alexander Technique.* Jerusalem, 1996.

Netter, Frank H., M.D. *The Atlas of Human Anatomy.* Ciba-Geigy Corp, New Jersey, 1989.

Nicholls, John. *The Alexander Technique, In Conversation with John Nicholls and Sean Carey.* Redwood Press Limited, UK, 1991.

Park, Glen. *The Art of Changing.* Ashgrove Press, Bath, England, 1989. Book and audio CD.

Parker, Andrew. *In the Blink of an Eye, How VISION sparked the big bang of evolution.* Basic books, NY, NY, 2003.

Paxton, Steve. *Material for the Spine*. Contredanse, Belgium, 2008.

Pert, Candace. *The Molecules of Emotion*. Scribner, New York, 1997.

Pierce, Alexandra & Pierce, Roger. *Expressive Movement—Posture and Action in Daily life, Sports and the Performing Arts*. Plenum Press, NY, NY, 1989.

Radinsky, Leonard B. *The Evolution of Vertebrate Design*. University of Chicago Press, 1987.

Robb, Fiona. *Not To Do*. Camon Press, London, 1999.

Roberts, Tristan. *Understanding Balance—the Mechanics of Posture and Locomotion*. Chapman & Hall, London, 1995.

Ruse, Michael editor with Joseph Travis. *Evolution, The First Four Billion Years*. Belknap Press of Harvard University Press, Forward by E.O. Wilson, 2009.

Shubin, Neil. *Your Inner Fish, A Journey into the 3.5 Billion-Year History of the Human Body*. Pantheon Books, NY, NY, 2008.

Shubin, Neil. *Your Inner Fish*. 3-part PBS series. Tangled Bank Studios, Windfall Films Ltd, 2014.

Staring, Jeroen. *Frederick Matthias Alexander 1869-1955. The Origins and History of the Alexander Technique*. Werkgroep Integrerende Wetenschapsbeoefening, Nijmegen, Netherlands, 2005.

Stevens, C.H. *Alexander Technique*. Optima, London, 1987.

Stevens, Christopher. *The F.M. Alexander Technique: Medical and Physiological Aspects*. 2nd edition, 1994.

Tasker, Irene. *Connecting Links*. Sheildrake Press, London, 1978.

Thompson, Lester with Richard A Brown. *The Scientific and Humanistic Contributions of Frank Pierce Jones on the F. Matthias Alexander Technique*. Based on papers presented at the 1st international Congress in 1986. Centerline Press, California, 1988.

Tobias, Phillip V. *Man, the Tottering Biped—The Evolution of his Posture, Poise and Skill*. Adept Printing Ltd. Bankstown, NSW, 1982.

Todd, Mabel Elsworth. *The Hidden You*. Dance Horizons, NY, 1953.

Todd, Mabel Elsworth. *The Thinking Body*. Dance Horizons, NY, 1939.

Travis, Joseph editor with Michael Ruse. *Evolution, The First Four Billion Years*. Belknap Press of Harvard University Press, Forward by E.O. Wilson. 2009.

Westfeldt, Lulie. *F. Matthias Alexander: The Man and his Work*. Centerline Press, Long Beach, CA, 1986.

Wielopolska, Kitty. *Never Ask Why, The live-adventure of Kitty Wielopolska as told to Joe Armstrong*. Novis Publications, Denmark, 2001.

Wright, Ben and Ed Bouchard. *Kinesthetic Ventures Informed by the Work of F.M Alexander, Stanislavski, Pierce & Freud*. Edited by Michael Protzel. Mesa Press, Chicago. 1997.

Magazine Articles and Newspaper Stories sorted by author.

Ackerman, Jennifer. "The Downside of Upright." *National Geographic*, July, 2006.

Ballard, Kathleen. "The Alexander Technique and Postural Reflexes." *The Congress Papers* (Brighton, England. August 1988), edited by Jeremy Chance. 35-39.

Barlow, Marjory. "The Ashley Place Bombing," letter to editor. *Direction V.2, #5*, 1994. p.33.

Blanc, Pamela. "Interview with Frank Ottiwell, the early years." *AmSAT News #67*, Spring 2005.

Bower, Bruce. "Consciousness in the Raw, The Brainstem May Orchestrate the Basics of Awareness." *Science News*, Sept. 15, 2007.

Bower, Bruce. "Walking Tall, Upright Evolution in Trees." *Science News*, August 4, 2007. 72-73.

Brenner, William. "Practical Marj." *Austat Journal, Vol. 1, #2.*

Brownlee, C. "Flies 'R' Us." *Science News*, September 2004. 180-181.

Carroll, Sean. "The Discover Interview with Sean Carroll." conducted by Pamela Weintraub. *Discover*, March 2009. 40-44.

Chen, Ingfei, "Born to Run." *Discover,* May, 2006. 62-67.

Coghill, G. "Amblystoma." 1929, the MacMillan Co.

Coghill, G. *Anatomy and the Problems of Behavior.* NY. Lecture delivered at the University in London.

Cohen, Bonnie Bainbridge. "The Dancer's Warm-up." *Contact Quarterly*, Fall, 1988. 32-33.

Cohen, Rivka. "The Primary Control: Some Personal Views." *AmSAT News #46*, 2000. 8-9.

Cranz, Galen. "What Do We Mean by the Head in the Alexander Technique?" AmSAT's FM *Alexander Memorial Address*, June 30, 2013. *AmSAT Journal #4*, Fall 2013. 52-57.

Crenson, Matt. "How We Run." *Salt Lake Tribune*, Jan. 11, 1996. p. C-1

Dart, Raymond. "An Anatomist's Tribute to the Alexander Technique." *STAT Memorial Lecture* March 20, 1970, Shieldrake Press, 1970.

de Alcantara, Pedro. "Whack! Smack! Ka-POW! Teaching Alexander Technique as a Martial Art." *AmSAT News #77*, 2008. 20-26.

de Peyer, Eric. *The Alexander Technique and its Value in Back Disorders.* 9-page pamphlet. STAT Books, London, 1963.

de Peyer, Eric. *Posture, Habit and Health.* 8-page pamphlet, publication of the Isobel Cripps Center, London, 1948.

Diamond, Joan. "The Israeli Directors, Five Portraits." *Direction V.2, #5*, 1994. 19-28.

Dimon, Ted. "The Organization of Movement, Four Talks on the Primary Control." *AmSAT Journal* Spring 2013-Fall 2014.

Dimon, Ted. "In Form and Moving: The Pelvic Girdle." Part V on a series on anatomical design and Function. *AmSAT News #49*. Fall, 2000.

Fertman, Bruce. "The Gift Given." *Peacefulbodyschool.com* 7/7/14.

Fox, Douglas. "Consciousness in a ... Cockroach?" *Discover Magazine,* January, 2007. 67-69

Frederick, Michael D. "Elisabeth Walker, A Life in Balance." *AmSAT Journal* Spring, 2014. 11-16.

Garlic, Dr. David. "Gravity and Posture." Nastat 1995 Annual Meeting Keynote Address. *Nastat News.* 10-11

Garlic, David. "The Garlick Report." *Direction V.2 #2*. Australia, 1994. p.5

Gorman, David. *Thinking about Thinking about Ourselves,* 1984 STAT Memorial Lecture.

Gray, John. "We Might Be able to Help." *Direction V.2, #2,* 1994. p.23.

Hauser-Wagner, Michaela with Giora Pinkas and Ruth Rootberg. "I Stand Corrected: Interview with Giora Pinkas." *AmSAT Journal* Spring, 2013.

Hoffman, Paul. "Circus Science." *Discover* cover story, Feb. 1996. 56-63.

Hogan, Kay. "The Ear and the Alexander Technique: Sound is Movement." *AmSAT News,* Spring, 2006. 22-24.

Huebner, Elizabeth. "Ann Sickels Mathews in Her Own Words" with Ann Mathews, and Phyllis G. Richmond. *AmSAT News* Winter, 2007. 21-25

Hunter, John. "Erika Whittaker." *AmSAT News,* Fall, 2004. p.12.

Jolley, Meg. "Mind in motion: A look into how and why 'The right thing does itself'." *AmSAT News #81,* Winter, 2009.

Jones, Frank Pierce. Lecture given at Indiana University School of Music Bloomington, Ind, 1975.

Jones, Frank Pierce. "A New Field for Inquiry." *Collected Writings on the Alexander Technique.* Alexander Technique Archives, Inc, 1948.

Kaminitz, Shoshana. "Mr. Macdonald." *Direction V.2, #5,* 1994. 6-10.

Kaminitz, Shoshana. "On Putting the Record Straight and More." *AmSAT News,* Spring, 2004. 20-21.

Kornfeld, Annie. "Jean Clark's Dart Work." *STAT News,* Jan. 2001

Kunzig, Robert. "Falling Forward." *Discover,* July 2001.

Liebowitz, Judith. "The Alexander Technique." *AmSAT Journal #3. Spring 2013.* 40-42..

Lovejoy, Owen C. "Evolution of Human Walking." *Scientific American,* November, 1988. 118-126.

Maffly, Brian. "Why Can Humans Run Great Distances?" University of Utah Biologist asks. *The Salt Lake Tribune*, February 14, 2009.

Magnus, Rudolf. "Physiology of Posture." Delivered at the University of Edinburgh, May 19 & 20, 1926.

Mathews, Ann. "Ann Sickels Mathews in Her Own Words" with Elizabeth Huebner and Phyllis G. Richmond. *AmSAT News* Winter 2007. 21-25

Mathews, Troup H. "Blessed Helicity." *Direction Journal V.1 #8.* Jeremy Chance, editor. 1991.

McKenna, Marjean. "Evolution, Ki, and the Aikidoka's Axis." *Contact Quarterly Vol. 34.1* Winter 2009/2010.

McMeekin, Jesse. "How the Leopard Got So Supple." *www.breakingmuscle.com/mobility-recovery/how-the-leopard-got-so-supple*

Monastersky, Richard. "Fossil Enigma Bares Teeth, Tells its Tale." *Science News Vol. 147,* April 29, 1995. p.261.

Monastersky, Richard. "The Road to a Backbone." *Science News Vol. 149* cover story, Feb. 3, 1996. 74-76.

Monastersky, Richard. "Waking Up to the Dawn of Vertebrates." *Science News Vol. 156,* Nov.6, 1999. p.292.

Morton, William. "Mr Scott (1918-1978)." *Direction. V.2, #5,* 1994. 11-13.

Murdoch, A. "The Function of the Sub-occipital Muscles. The Key to Posture, Use and Functioning." Paper read 5/5/1936 for the BMA.

Murray, Alex. "The Dart Procedures." *Direction. Vol.1, #3.* May, 1988.

Nash, Madeleine. "When Life Exploded." *Time,* Dec. 4, 1995. 66-74.

Nelson, Lisa and Nancy Stark Smith. "Perceiving in Action, Interview with Bonnie Bainbridge Cohen." *Contact Quarterly* Spring/Summer 1984.

Nicholls, Lynn. "Dilys Carrington as Interpreted by Lynn Nicholls."

Nickolaus, Melanie Rae. "Dr. Christopher Hubert Howard Stevens." *AmSAT News,* Summer 2004.

Nott, Adam. "Issue editorial." *Direction Magazine V2 #2,* 1994. p. 4.

Ottiwell, Frank. "Interview with Frank Ottiwell, the early years." by Pamela Blanc. *AmSAT News #67,* Spring 2005.

Ottiwell, Frank. "Nastat's 1st Annual F.M. Alexander Memorial Lecture." *Nastat News,* 1989. 8-9.

Ottiwell, Frank. "The Alexander Technique: A Matter of Choice." *Your Body Works,* 1980. 65-71

Owen, Edward H. "The Man Who Mastered Habit." First printed in *EROS Magazine*, 1955. Reprinted 1956 by Sheildrake Press and recently by Mornum Time Press for AmSAT. (www.amsitonline.org)

Oxford, Frances. "Marjorie Barstow Interviewed." *Direction V2, #2.* 1994.

PBS 4-part series, *Australia's First Four Billion Years*, 2013

Pennisi, E. "Vertebrates' Cousin Shares Key Genes." *Science News, Vol. 146.* Aug. 20, 1994. p. 116.

Peterson, Ivars. "Shadows and Symmetries." *Science News, Vol. 140.* Dec. 21 & 28, 1991. 408-410.

Pinkas, Giora with Ruth Rootberg and Michaela Hauser-Wagner. "I Stand Corrected: Interview with Giora Pinkas." *AmSAT Journal* Spring 2013.

Richmond, Phyllis G. "Ann Sickels Mathews in Her Own Words" with Ann Mathews and Elizabeth Huebner. *AmSAT News* Winter 2007. 21-25.

Richmond, Phyllis. "The Alexander Technique and Dance." *The Alexander Journal #11*, Spring 1991. 19-28.

Rickover, Robert. "Viewpoint." *Direction V.2, #2*, 1994. p.34.

Rickover, Robert. "Viewpoint." *Direction V.2, #5*, 1994. p.34.

Rootberg, Ruth with Giora Pinkas and Michaela Hauser-Wagner. "I Stand Corrected: Interview with Giora Pinkas." *AmSAT Journal* Spring 2013.

Rosenthal, Eleanor. "Judith Liebowitz: Her Legacy." *The Congress Papers, Engelberg, Switzerland.* Direction, NSW Australia, 1991. 24-30.

Schwartz, John. "Can Smiles Trigger Brain Response?" *The Washington Post*, 1993

Schirle, Joan. Editor, *The Newsletter of ACAT West. V. 1, #2*, May, 1986.

Sendowski, Shulamit. "Daring to Change—an interview with Judith Stransky." *AmSAT Journal* Spring 2014. 43-49.

Sherrington, Sir Charles. "The Brain and its Mechanism." Cambridge University Press, 1937. via *The Alexander Journal #7*, Spring 1972. p.30.

Stark Smith, Nancy. "Moving from Within." Interview with Bonnie Bainbridge Cohen. *Naropa Magazine*. 1983.

Stark Smith, Nancy and Lisa Nelson. "Perceiving in Action, Interview with Bonnie Bainbridge Cohen." *Contact Quarterly* Spring/summer 1984.

Stevens, Dr. Christopher H.H. "New Developments in the Alexander Technique." *AmSAT News #64.* 23-25.

Stillwell, Janet O'Brien. "Interview with Marjorie L. Barstow." *Somatics*, 1981. 15-21.

Strickler, Jeff. "95-year-old shares tricks of safe falling." *Star Tribune,* March 2, 2015.

Taubes, Gary. "Conversations in a Cell." *Discover*, Feb. 1996. 49-54.

Tinbergen, Nikolaas. "Ethology and Stress Diseases: An Examination of the Alexander Technique." *Science Vol. 185* cover story, July 5, 1974. 20-27. Nobel Oration reprinted with permission from the Nobel Foundation .

Travis, John. "The Ghost of Geoffroy Saint-Hillaire." *Science News, Vol. 148.* Sept. 30, 1995. 216-218.

Trevelyan, Sir George. "Act — Don't React." *Direction, V.1 #5.* 164-170.

Trevelyan, Sir George. "The True Wholeness." *The Alexander Journal #13* Autumn 1993. 23-30.

Travis, John. "Dialing up an Embryo." *Science News Vol. 154,* Aug 15, 1998.

Walker, Elizabeth. "Fifty Five Years On." *Direction V.2 #2,* 1994. p.30.

Walsh, Nanette. "Peggy Williams." *AmSAT News*, Spring 2004. p.16.

Webster, Mark. "A Tale of Two Trainings." *Direction V.2 #5,* 1994. p.15.

Weintraub, Pamela. "The Discover Interview with Sean Carroll." *Discover*, March 2009. p.40-44.

Whittaker, Erika Schumann. "Alexander's Way." *The Alexander Journal #13*, Autumn 1993. 3-12.

Wielopolska, Kitty. "The Discovery and the Use of the Eye Order in Teaching the Alexander Work." From a talk Mario Passaglini and Wielopolska gave to *ACAT* in NYC. Edited by Carol Attwood.

Zimmer, Carl. "Coming on to the Land." *Discover*, June, 1995.

Zimmer, Carl. "A Fin is a Limb is a Wing - How Evolution Fashioned its Masterworks." *National Geographic*, Nov. 2006. 111-127; 134-135.

Zimmer, Carl. "No Skycaps Needed." *Discover,* August, 1995.

Zimmer, Carl. "The Purpose of Toes." *Discover*, February, 1995. p. 32.

We tend to think we know how to move better than our bodies do, so with all good intentions, we interfere with our *use*. Repetition of our interference strengthens the *misuse*. It is not possible to "do" *good use*—it happens by itself when we do not interfere with it.

– Phyllis Richmond

CREDITS

for Photos and Illustrations

With Table of Contents

Marjean guides Christopher into a walk. Drawing by Christopher Neville.

Introduction

Alexa Green and Lou Hickman, light on their feet. Photos presumably by respective parents.

Chapter 1

Rover's primary axis adapted from a 2015 cartoon drawing by Brian Basset. ©Universal Uclick.

The Primary Axis. Marjean lying down with calves on seat of a chair. Illustration by Christopher Neville.

Chordate ancestors. Drawing by Christopher Neville.

Animals (lion, bear, gorilla, seabiscuit and tarsier) illustrated by Christopher Neville.

Leatherback tortoise drawing by Christopher Neville after photo © Brian Skerry/National Geographic Creative.

Greater flamingos taking flight drawn by Christopher Neville after a photo by Roy Toft of National Geographic Creative.

Golfer Adam Scott sketch by Christopher Neville.

Hall of fame quarterback Joe Montana sketched by Christopher Neville after a photograph by Walter Iooss Jr. © Sports Illustrated/Getty Images.

Jackie Joyner-Kersee 1995 long jump, © AP Photo/Lynne Sladky.

Rafael Nadal illustration by Christopher Neville after a photograph by Fred Vuich. © Sports Illustrated/Getty Images.

Haeckel's 1874 chart of comparative vertebrate embryos taken from the internet.

Fetus in the womb and crawling baby drawings by Christopher Neville from images online.

Chapter 2

Okamoto Yoko Shihan, 6th Dan, preparing to lead an aikido class. 2014 Documentary celebrating Aikido Kyoto and Nishijin Dojo. Drawing by Christopher Neville from an image procured from youtube.

Primate branch-walking. Image procured from the internet.

Sketches by Christopher Neville showing the central nerve cord and brainstem and the relationship of the head to the neck/back.

Madagascar monkey (Propithecus coronatus) illustrated by Alfred Grandidier. Photo by J. Beckett. © J. Beckett / American Museum of Natural History.

The foramen ovale, three viewpoints. Drawing by Christopher Neville.

Skull with *forward and up* directions illustrated by Christopher Neville.

Toddler running with legs tagging along. Drawing by Christopher Neville.

Prince George with brainpan as high up as possible. Drawn by Christopher Neville from a Parade Magazine photo.

Prone infant with eyes as high as possible and brainpan level. Photo from McKenna family archives.

San Francisco Giants' Tim Lincecum triptych
-Sliding 2011 Spring Training. © Jed Jacobsohn/Sports Illustrated/Getty Images.
-Pitching in World Series game 5 vs Texas Rangers. © 2010 Robert Beck/Sports Illustrated/Getty Images.
-Pitching vs Kansas City 7/7/2008. © Mike Powell/Sports Illustrated/Getty Images.

Roger Federer in semifinal of US Open vs Novak Djokovic. 9/6/2008 © Bob Martin/Sports Illustrated/Getty Images.

Philadelphia Eagles' quarterback Michael Vick at Soldier Field in Chicago 11/28/2010. © Photo by Drew Hallowell/Philadelphia Eagles/Getty Images.

Haile Selassie, President of Ethiopia for decades, from Wikipedia Commons.

Shay Paulsmeyer and Arthur Rubinstein showing occiputs in line with the rest of their backs. Illustrations by Christopher Neville.

Two versions of pulling the head back and down drawn by Christopher Neville from images online.

Chief Manuelito, native American Indian chief Hastiin Ch'il Haajiní, from Wikipedia Commons.

Sri Yukteswar, Hindu sage, from Wikipedia Commons.

African boy with occiput behind the the rest of the back, illustrated by Christopher Neville.

Meercats © Chris Johns/National Geographic Creative.

Prairie Dog photo © Mattias Klum/National Geographic Creative.

Drawings of *poor use* of the model and military posture by Christopher Neville from images online.

Jeremy Duncan from Zits cartoon illustrated by Jim Borgman. ©ZITS © 2000. Zits Partnership, Dist. by King Features.

Chapter 3

Marjean moving from sitting into a crawl illustrated by Christopher Neville.

Babies crawling photos from the internet &/or drawings by Christopher Neville.

Man and baby crawling. Illustrates the arch of the arms and upper back. Drawing by Christopher Neville.

Baby in overalls crawling. Photo from the internet.

Even while standing, is crawling an option? Marjean giving Christopher a chair lesson. Drawing by Christopher Neville.

Chapter 4

Alexander in New York City in 1916. Unable to obtain permission. © unknown. Taken from page 159 of J.A. Evans' *Frederick Matthias Alexander - a Family History* published in 2001 by Phillimore & Co., Ltd., which was acquired in 2003 by London based The History Press.

Photograph of FM Alexander teaching with hands on man's back. © 2015 The Society of Teachers of the Alexander Technique, London.

Photograph of FM Alexander teaching child while sitting in a chair. © 2015 The Society of Teachers of the Alexander Technique, London.

Portrait of FM Alexander, 1941. © 2015 The Society of Teachers of the Alexander Technique, London.

Chapter 5

A chair lesson with Alexander. Photograph of FM Alexander © 2015 The Society of Teachers of the Alexander Technique, London.

"Forward and Up" drawing, repeated from Chapter 2 by Christopher Neville.

A chair lesson. Sketch by Christopher Neville.

Christopher taking a lesson from Marjean, two photos from Marjean's computer.

No pulling head back and down sketched by Christopher Neville.

Judith Stern lures Eileen Troberman into a spiral as she rises from a chair during an AmSAT conference in 2006.

Chapter 6

Ozzie Smith does his famous backflip during the 1985 World Series. Photo by Ronald C. Modra/Sports Illustrated/Getty Images.

The *sitting tripod* by Christopher Neville.

The *sitting cone* by Christopher Neville.

African woman walks while carrying a basket of fruit on her head. Drawing by Christopher Neville from an image acquired from the internet.

Anton's contralateral. Photo by Marjean McKenna.

Chris Evert and Steffi Graf demonstrate their terrific monkeys. Drawings by Christopher Neville from composite sources.

Baseball players and a lemur demonstrating their similar *monkeys*. Drawings by Christopher Neville.

Monkey illustrations by Christopher Neville.

Roz Newmark fiddles in *monkey*, drawing by Christopher Neville after a photo by Roz.

Andre Agassi French Open Final 1999. Photo by Patrick Kovarik/AFP/Getty Images.

Charles Barkley 1992 All Star Game. Photo by Jon Soohoo/NBAE via Getty Images.

Prince in *monkey* while playing guitar during the halftime of the 2007 Superbowl. © photo by Jeff Kravitz/FilmMagic, Inc./Getty Images.

FM Alexander in lunge. © 2015 The Society of Teachers of the Alexander Technique, London.

Marjean in lunge while giving a lesson.

Squatting African woman with child bathing. © Nevada Wier/CORBIS 1999

Four squatting toddlers. Anton's photo (lower left) by Marjean McKenna. Other sources unidentified.

Folding into a crawl illustration by Christopher Neville.

Crawlers illustrated by Christopher Neville.

Getting up from a crawl illustrations by Christopher Neville.

Skeleton showing *semi-supine position* illustrated by Christopher Neville after a similar drawing in Glen Park's *The Art of Changing*.

Bonobo in semi-supine. Photo by Takeshi Furuichi.

The *pelvic tilt* drawn by Christopher Neville.

Semi-supine = *monkey* rotated 90°. Three images illustrated by Christopher Neville.

"Katelyn Lloyd hurdles in the halls of Rich High School" illustrated by Christopher Neville after a 2010 photograph by Jim Urquhart in the Salt Lake Tribune.

Three gangly youths as published in Michael Gelb's *Body Learning*. Permissions unavailable—image available from internet.

Two *Eustace Tilley* images on 2015 *New Yorker* anniversary covers, "Nine for Ninety." *Good use* by Kadir Nelson and *poor use* by Carter Goodrich; © Conde Nast.

Peanuts cartoon by Charles Schultz. © UniversalUClick.

Young boy slouching at his school desk photo from the internet.

Gabby slouching on couch in *Grand Avenue* comic strip by Steve Breen. ©UniversalUclick

Cartoon figures showing *misuse* in upright locomotion. Permission from Direction Journal. 2015 Website.

Cartoon figures showing *misuse* in sitting by Christopher Neville.

Chapter 7

Tensegrity structure image © David Gorman, with permission. From *Looking at Ourselves*.

The brainpan likes to be level drawing by Christopher Neville.

The *pulley image* as sketched by Christopher Neville.

The *whole back* from three viewpoints by Christopher Neville.

The *atlas and the axis* as sketched by Christopher Neville.

Payson's Aerial by Susie Fitzhugh. 1974.

The *pelvic arch* with sit bones and femur labeled. Sketched by Christopher Neville.

The *foot pyramid* sketched by Christopher Neville.

The ball and socket joint joining the femur to the hip.

Merce Cunningham performing in 1970. Photo by James Klotsky.

Tango dancers demonstrate the spiral. Photo from the internet.

Golfer Rory McIlroy demonstrates a spiral from the soles of his feet to the back of his eyes. Photo by Kohjiro Kinno. ©Sports Illustrated/Getty Images, 2014.

The spirals of the outer musculature by Christopher Neville after drawings in Raymond Dart's *Skill & Poise*, p.69.

The double helix of the deep spiral postural muscles. © Elsevier/Thomas W. Meyers' *Anatomy Trains*, p.138.

Photograph of FM Alexander helping a toddler to suspend his body from his head. © 2015 The Society of Teachers of the Alexander Technique, London.

Roz Newmark leaping. Photo by Roz Newmark.

Leaping cat © photo by Marion Duckworth Smith.

Chapter 8

All drawings by Christopher Neville.

The whole back illustration by Christopher Neville adapted from a *Gray's Anatomy* illustration by Henry Vandyke Carter.

Upright *use* with cane, Utah pictograph from Utah rock art.

The Senses Game photograph from the internet.

Photograph of FM Alexander 'checking for messages.' © 2015 The Society of Teachers of the Alexander Technique, London.

Runner Ryan Hall © Martin Schoeller/AUGUST.

Taiji sparring, Ed Young and Tam Gibbs in NYC. © via Media Publishing Company 1999; photograph courtesy of Ed Young/McIntosh & Otis, Inc.

Appendix 1 - Quotes

Alexander the orator. Photograph of FM Alexander © 2015 The Society of Teachers of the Alexander Technique, London.

Marjory Barlow and Marj Barstow at 1988 International Congress. Image used with permission from *Direction Journal, Vol.1 #5, The Congress Issue.*

Marjory and Wilfred Barlow celebrating the 1973 publication of his book, *The Alexander Principle.* Image used with permission from *Direction Journal, Vol.2, #2, The Barlows Issue.*

Dilys Carrington photo taken by Susan Martin Cohen.

Walter Carrington. Image used with permission from *Direction Journal, Vol.1, #4, The Walter Carrington Issue.* P.127.

Patrick Macdonald - photo reprinted with permission from the Patrick Macdonald Archive.

Dick and Elisabeth Walker, during their training in the late 1930's atop Crib Goch in North Wales. Image used with permission from *Direction Journal, Vol.2, #2, The Barlows Issue.* p.29.

Bob Britton showing the way, 2010. © Louise Gauld

The author with Marj Barstow and Frank Ottiwell at the 2nd International Congress in Brighton, England, 1988. Photo by Eric Eliason.

FM with John Dewey c.1920. © 2015 The Society of Teachers of the Alexander Technique, London.

Pamela Blanc 1979 graduation photo, © Pamela Blanc. Photo probably by Paul Broucek.

Chair photograph from the Denver Art Museum.

Appendix 2, Cartoons, Photos, Images.

Sky hook image, revised version drawn by Christopher Neville.

Use and Function cartoon reproduced with permission from *Direction Journal*.

Joan Murray leads Gray Sutton into the *hands on back of chair* procedure with a deep, anthropoidal *monkey*. © Alexander Technique Center Urbana.

The Whole Barrel = the primary axis. Drawings by Christopher Neville.

July 5, 1974 *Science* Magazine cover reprinted with permission from AAAS. Drawings from *The Alexander Principle* by Wilfred Barlow (Copyright © Wilfred Barlow, 1973) and reprinted by permission of A.M. Heath & Co Ltd.

Comparative spinal processes from Tobias' *Man the Tottering Biped*: © the estate of Phillip V. Tobias.

Comparative girth and direction of suboccipital muscles. Reproduced from Phillip V. Tobias' *Man, The Tottering Biped* with permission from Borntraeger Press, Berlin. www.schweizerbart. de © Borntrager / 1932 Theodor Mollison.

Picture of Celine Dion. Source unknown.

Poor use of cane, Utah pictograph from Utah rock art.

Drawings of bad *use* by Christopher Neville

Poor use demonstration by man and boy, a stillshot the movie *Slingblade*. Photo from internet.

Slingblade cartoon © Jon Agee/The New Yorker Collection/The Cartoon Bank.

Various Advertisements, various sources.

For Better or For Worse cartoon by Lynn Johnston. © UniversalUclick

Speed Chutes photo of Denver Bronco's training camp from *Sports Illustrated*, 1990s. No permissions.

Appendix 3, Further Reading

Rose Bronec leads Mara Sokolsky into a crawl, 2010. © Louise Gauld.

Glossary

Think a smile. Archaic Greek statue, Tête de Cavalier. © RMN-Grand Palais/Art Resource, NY.

About the Author

Marjean at approximately age 12 from the Maurer family archives.
Marjean getting *direction* from Marj Barstow around 1990.

Acknowledgements

I thank, above all, illustrator, artistic designer, producer, and collaborator Christopher Neville, for making this happen—for almost three years of bi-weekly meetings bringing "droplets of attention" to the book, which had been on the back burner too long. It was 2006 when I first approached him about being my artist. He had undreamed of other skills from computer wizard techno geek to terrific tango practice partner. Christopher edited, too, in a producerly way. It has been a collaboration of a lifetime.

Ann Schwarz, my oldest best friend and personal editor, had at one point either written or rewritten almost every sentence of this book. Her insistence on succinct brevity trimmed ideas to their essence. In high school Ann and I had worked together on our award-winning newspaper staff; now we rendezvous to hike in the desert every year or two. Over the years, with only an occasional lesson from me and others, Ann has absorbed a lot about the AT and made big preemptive changes in the *use of herself*. She has lobbied for this book since I began training to become an Alexander teacher.

Terry Surguine, also a friend since junior high school, insisted a year ago on volunteering to be a co-editor. He is a recently retired strategic communications professional who wanted to contribute more to the book than just be a reader. Terry always saw the big picture as well as the tiniest details. He figuratively held my hand through times of despair, wisely counseling me to chill—that the book *needed* to percolate. Together he and Ann have been an irreplaceable team that has guided my original garbled manuscript to something simple and coherent.

Toby Lafferty was an editor ex-officio. Good friend and confidante, this ex-university professor took me page by page through her annotations of early drafts. Toby and I have "played in the sandbox" since 2003, with me assisting her handyperson profession—from building fences to painting my house while solving the world's problems and trading a few AT lessons along the way. She has persistently encouraged me to "get writing."

For decades Roz Newmark has been a mental backboard for ideas about mind/body/spirit. She was my first Alexander student, waiting for a teacher to come to SLC; she made several contributions to my teaching vocabulary. We have shared annual play days: XC skiing, hiking, neighborhood walks, and chat sessions discussing our shared interest in movement, our families, and our multiple intersecting circles of friends.

Tami Derezotes is one of those shared friends. With well over 100 lessons, many in trade for her seamstress talents, Tami knows most of my verbiage by heart. Her presence and prescient support have buoyed me up through times of difficulty and doubt.

I thank my SLC taiji family, whom I see every week. Especially Barbara Zakarian for our shared investigations into movement. She phones me intermittently to tell me her newest revelation about why *entertaining the notion of crawling* is so effective for her. I am eternally grateful to her for getting me into tango.

I thank high school journalism teacher, the late Jo Arnold, who taught me about brevity. I thank her for the entire school newspaper experience. She would have been a reader, had I not taken so long.

I thank Frank Ottiwell, my Alexander trainer at ATI-SF, for his kind depth, wisdom, and empathy. He was enthusiastic about my book-in-process and offered critical suggestions to early drafts to keep me out of hot water with my colleagues. In school he would share his own humbling insights into his ongoing process of change and discovery. He was forever curious about other approaches. By the time I arrived at his school, it had hosted first-generation teachers Patrick Macdonald and Walter and Dilys Carrington for the last time, but Marj Barstow continued to visit.

I thank all of the teachers on Frank's training course during my time there: Rome Roberts Earle, Larry Ball, Simone Biase, Bob Britton, Gloria Gotti, Jerry Sontag, Carol Gill, Gail Felbain, and librarian savant, John Coffin. I thank visiting teachers: Deborah Caplan, Jeremy Chance, Barbara Conable, Bruce Fertman, Shaike Hermelin, Alain Jacques, Kelly McEvenue, and Mio Morales.

Marj Barstow was my first Alexander teacher, known for her emphasis on "constructive thinking." Her influence was apparent in many of my teachers and is reflected in the quotes appendix of this book.

Troup Mathews, whom I met in Lincoln at a Marj Barstow New Year's workshop, generously gave me my first private lesson in his room at the YMCA (floor lesson—Troup's prosthetic leg 'n all), which convinced me that this was to become my life's work. For years I thought I would be training with him. Later I bonded also with his wife, Ann, with whom I shared ideas about developmental movement.

I want to give special thanks to readers Ann Schwarz, Terry Surguine, Toby Lafferty, and Christopher Neville, who read every draft and to Kari Prindl, who offered detailed suggestions early on. Every reader saw different things—some, particularly Alexander teachers like Bob Britton, Mara Sokolsky, Clare Maxwell, and Elizabeth Huebner asked for clarification of my words, concepts, and ideas. Thanks to Mara for the book's title. Clare and Roz Newmark both suggested improvement to stylistic and artistic detail like standardizing fonts and chapter headings and properly framing photos.

Eagle eyed Maya Christopherson and Linda Reed both caught tiny spelling and punctuation errors that nobody else (including two spell-check programs) saw. Karen Nelson and Ken McKenna offered valuable improvements to the text and both were insistent that I get more politically correct with my pronouns. Michal Lahav and Tami Derezotes offered encouragement and valuable feedback on multiple fronts. Lay readers Blaine Lam and Jack McKenna appreciated the hints for lifetime well-being. Their praise of the quotes appendix convinced me to retain it. Each reader offered insights and suggestions that made the book better. Other readers were Pat McGinnis, Frank Ottiwell, and Steve Paxton.

I thank all of my classmates at ATI-SF and my Utah Alexander colleagues, Jacque Bell and Cathy Pollock. (Cathy's actually in the Tetons now.) Jacque's gem of a husband, Bart, should get a quick mention here, too.

I thank Alexander colleagues worldwide with whom I have bonded, especially Willa Allen, Regula Bayer, Pamela Blanc, Robin Bowie, Diana Bradley, Bob Britton, Rose Bronec, Ronit Corry, Steve Corry, Ron Dennis, Mary Eagle, Rome Roberts Earle, Missy Vineyard Erdgood, Lisa First, Dinah Goodes, Elizabeth Huebner, Debby Jay, Glenn Kenreich, Noel Kingsley, Sumi Komo, Clare Maxwell, Patricia McInnis, Ben Miller, Linda Newton, Karin O'Flanagan, Flora Ojanen, Giora Pinkas, Cheryl Pleskow, Kari Prindl, Merran Poplar, Bobby Rosenberg, Rosa Schramm, Mara Sokolsky, Eileen Troberman, Deborah Weitzman, Camillo Vacalabre, and Paula Zacharias.

I am indebted to my first dance teachers, Marsha Paludan, Nancy Topf, and John Rolland, who indirectly led me to the Alexander Technique through the work of Barbara Clark and Mabel Todd; Bonnie Bainbridge Cohen for her investigations into developmental movement and cellular consciousness; Steve Paxton for "finding" *contact improvisation* and for encouraging me to write; and Joan and Alex Murray for their part in the creation, exploration, and dissemination of the *Dart Procedures*. Special thanks to David Gorman for the generosity of his time and the clarity of his writing, which helped me finally understand *tensegrity*. I am grateful to all who granted me permission to use their photographs.

I thank close friends and fellow movement investigators: Julie Calhoun, Natalie Clausen, Maya Christopherson, Tami Derezotes, Michal Lahav, Jess Humphrey, Toby Lafferty, Adwoa Lemieux, Gabriela Morales, Karen Nelson, Roz Newmark, Linda Reed, Sally Van Dusen, and Barbara Zakarian.

I thank Becky and Kent Douglass, lifelong friends who have always supported me; ex-business partners and long-time friends Jude Rubadue, Curtis Mays, and Orian Collinsworth; ex-husbands, Peter and Eric; parents, siblings, and McDowell cousins.

Finally, I pay tribute to over 100 years of people interpreting Alexander's work, which has become richer.

On the left Marjean at approximately age 12 and on the right, in her mid 40's with Marj Barstow.

About the Author

Once a graduate student in embryology and later a professional skier, Marjean took her first Alexander lesson in 1976 and certified as a teacher in 1990 (ATI-SF). Marjean is especially interested in evodevo (evolutionary developmental biology), comparative anatomy, and developmental movement. Her movement passions include the martial arts, taiji and aikido, in which she holds a second-degree black belt, contact improvisation, and tango. She likes to walk and loves to hike in the canyons of southern Utah.

A Utahn since 1970, Marjean lives in Salt Lake City.

About the Illustrator

Christopher Neville was born to goodly parents in the latter day province of Provo, Utah. From there he has managed to see most of the continents on the planet and to meet more people than he can manage. He firmly believes that we were given this opportunity of life to learn the lesson of service. But it wasn't until he tangoed into Marjean and subsequently the Alexander Technique that he learned what preceded service. He says about his experience with the technique: "To soothe someone in pain is commendable. But to manually reconfigure the psycho-physical system to be unable to hold it any longer is an ability that heretofore I've only seen come from plants."

Christopher also lives, eats, drinks and dances in Salt Lake City and can finally stand babies.

Made in the USA
Middletown, DE
19 January 2017